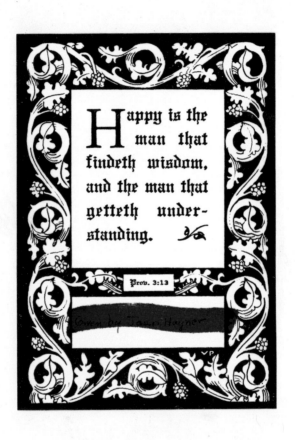

Happy is the man that findeth wisdom, and the man that getteth under-standing.

Prov. 3:13

Given by Jauri Hayner

4 05

COMMANDOS for CHRIST

Harper Jungle Missionary Classics

HOMER E. DOWDY
> *Christ's Witchdoctor*

FRANK AND MARIE DROWN
> *Mission to the Head-Hunters*

ELISABETH ELLIOT
> *Through Gates of Splendor*
>
> *Shadow of the Almighty*
>
> *The Savage My Kinsman*

RUSSELL T. HITT
> *Jungle Pilot*
>
> *Cannibal Valley*

ETHEL EMILY WALLIS
> *The Dayuma Story*

COMMANDOS
for CHRIST

The Gospel Witness in
Bolivia's "Green Hell"

Bruce E. Porterfield

HARPER & ROW, PUBLISHERS

New York, Evanston, and London

To my friends who have a part in the ministry of reaching the many tribes with the Gospel message of our Lord Jesus Christ

Contents

	Foreword by William B. Young	7
1.	I AM CHALLENGED	11
2.	FACING THE UNKNOWN	17
3.	ON THE EDGE OF DARKNESS	33
4.	RECONNAISSANCE	40
5.	SPEARHEAD	54
6.	CATAPULTED INTO THE STONE AGE	67
7.	DIGGING IN	77
8.	NEW BEACHHEAD	84
9.	COMMANDO WIVES	96
	Picture section	97-112
10.	DUNKIRK OF THE SOUL	130
11.	GRIP OF THE SWAMP	147
12.	PERILOUS HOURS AND THE INNER VOICE	165
13.	A NEW FRONT: COMMANDOS FOR PEACE	182
14.	DESPERATE STAND AT THE STRONGHOUSE	210
15.	REGROUPING FOR VICTORY	230
	Acknowledgments	239

Foreword

Commandos for Christ is a book of great spiritual adventure. It deals with the realities of pioneer evangelism in the tribal areas of Bolivia. This book explains in detail the most hazardous work in the area of Christian responsibility. Risks are not carelessly incurred in efforts to carry the Good News of Salvation to dangerous killers in remote Indian tribes. Before perilous steps are taken, the cost is counted and possible martyrdom squarely faced.

This fascinating narrative of jungle thrusts is highly informative. It is inspirational. Readers will find joy in the midst of sorrow. Bruce Porterfield's sense of humor eases tensions in many tight spots. The faithfulness of God is recorded in the most unusual circumstances.

The words of the Lord to the first pioneer missionary have reached the heart of the author: ". . . I send thee, to open their eyes, and to turn them from darkness to light, and from the power of Satan unto God, that they may receive forgiveness of sins, and inheritance among them which are sanctified by faith that is in me" (Acts 26:17-18). The realization of this Divine Call has spurred Bruce Porterfield to ford swollen rivers, wade through swamps, and tread jungle trails by day and by night. Neither tropi-

7

cal diseases of the body, nor innumerable annoying insects, nor deadly reptiles, nor hunger, nor thirst could deter this determined soldier of Jesus Christ. His is an exhibition of the "love of Christ which constraineth." The author deserves the distinction of a missionary statesman.

Those who read this volume will be blessed with renewed vision. It will inspire greater participation in helping to carry out the program of God for world evangelization.

WILLIAM B. YOUNG
President of Worldwide Keswick*

* World-wide Keswick, originally founded in England in 1875, sponsors annual interdenominational conferences, distributes Protestant literature, and supports other nonsectarian Christian works throughout the world.

COMMANDOS for CHRIST

bracketed sections - for a missionary
    story

1

1 Am Challenged

As I fought my way along the overgrown trail, the temptation to turn back grew stronger and stronger. All the difficulties and miseries of my lonely situation crept through my mind like a poisonous vine. More and more I felt it had been foolhardy of me to try to make my way alone through this all-but-trackless "Green Hell" of jungle in the unexplored territory near the Bolivian border.

Here, in the midst of this steaming humidity, it was becoming impossible to find drinking water. I had been hiking steadily for four days and sweating continuously. By now it was near the middle of the afternoon. That meant I'd had my last drink about ten hours earlier. I could see no hope of finding more water soon, and my throat was parched from thirst.

My feet were covered with blisters, and the packstraps bit into my shoulders. I faltered, stopped for a minute, and tried to shift the straps to less painful spots.

Dizzily, I looked around me. I was in a relatively open place, a small grove of squat palm trees. Their rough trunks, a yard or more in diameter, rose like huge, moldering, brown corncobs to a height of about fifteen feet, at which point the branches spread out, heavy-laden with broad green leaves. Beyond the fat, spaced palms, the denser, vaster jungle trees stood like a living wall, rising to a height of sixty feet or more and sending their network of branches and vines to clasp together high above the palm leaves. I looked up, hoping to check on the weather, but saw only this impenetrable, imprisoning dome—there was no patch of sky.

The air was heavy and oppressive with the moldy odors of dying things. On the damp earth around me lay fallen palm branches and half-decayed leaves. Scattered ferns drooped listlessly in the humid heat. The broken, empty shells of palm nuts, their meat gouged from them by hungry animals, had been strewn over the clearing to rot and nourish the soil which had once nourished them. The brown skin of the earth was pockmarked where it had been recently grubbed and torn, exposing the ashen-gray soil beneath and at the edge of the holes protruded the bitten-off ends of dying roots, white as bones.

Common sense told me to turn back; an inner voice prodded me on. It was the same conflict I had been undergoing for the past three days. There was no practical reason anyone knew of for me to try to reach my friends now, in the dry season. For all I knew, they were safely encamped deep in the jungle, having ferried themselves and their adequate supplies by water into the Macurapi country when the swamps and the rivers were higher. And yet I had come this far. I had doggedly crossed the worst swamp I ever saw and trudged miles and miles through thick, endless jungle to try to reach them with a small supply of extra foods and medicines I felt they might need. Why?

Why? I asked myself this question for the hundredth time. And for the hundredth time the persistent urging voice from within came in reply: *Because—you must keep going.*

I began to imagine myself on a cool veranda, relaxing with a glass of ice tea in my hand . . .

Suddenly I was jolted to my senses by a fierce clacking sound. Directly in front of me, twenty feet ahead, stood a large, black, wild pig. He made the clacking sound with his gleaming white teeth, visible behind his rolled-back upper lip. This sound, and the shiny black bristles sticking out of the ugly black hide of his back, left me no doubt he was mad.

A second clacking joined the first: another pig was standing not five feet from him. With a shock of fear, I looked carefully and saw another, and another—four of them, all clacking at me with those vicious teeth.

I drew my pistol and slipped the safety button. Slowly, I began to back away. Out of the corners of my eyes I tried to pick out the nearest of the tall jungle trees to climb if I had to—the crumbling bark of the fat palms was impossible to scale.

The pigs stood their ground like sentries, stolid, massive, malevolent, their teeth clacking hungrily. I continued to inch backward, trying desperately to reckon the distance to the tree I had picked out, and balancing this against their probable speed.

Then directly in back of me, I heard a sharp clacking sound. I whirled. Half a dozen more of them blocked my path to the rear! They added their mad clackings to those of the pigs in front of me. Before I had time to make a break for the tree, a wall of sound exploded all around me. Heralded by the ghastly, clacking chorus, an army of shining black eyes, black bristles, and white teeth moved out of the jungle to bar my way in every direction. All climbable trees were now beyond their circle of ambush. They moved into a tight ring and halted, immovable, implacable, clacking furiously. With a quick, terrified check I estimated about seventy of them. I had nine shots in my pistol. Small help! If they charged, the weapon would prolong my life by thirty seconds at the most.

The nearest pigs were about twenty feet in front of me. They held their ground. I held my ground. Minutes ticked by. The clacking went on undiminished.

"Lord," I prayed, "I sure need help from You."

In this war of nerves, the noise itself was almost enough to unhinge me completely. Perhaps that was their tactic: to wait me out while they wore me down with that awful noise, waiting, and waiting, for that moment . . .

I had to do something. I tried inching forward. When I had moved about a foot, the pigs in front of me took a step back, moving together, as if by command. I took a full step. They took another step back. I looked behind me: the pigs there had moved up. I was now exactly two feet farther up the trail and in exactly the same situation. The clacking went on unbearably—their tactic was beginning to work on me. I was alone and defenseless.

They had me.

What a chain of events had led up to this moment—nine years of them, in fact! During World War II I had received a medical discharge from the Navy. I went to work in a war plant in Lansing, Michigan, and knew I was unhappy, though I was not sure why. I did know that for three years I had had thoughts about becoming a missionary, but steadily tried to put them out of my mind. Working in a factory was not really what I wanted, but I couldn't see any other immediate possibilities.

At the end of every day, I would go home exhausted—not only from the hard work, but from frustration, too. I was not doing what I wanted to do nor what I should be doing. But I would not face the growing challenge within; I fought against it. Perhaps I was afraid I lacked the faith and dedication necessary for missionary work.

One bleak January evening in 1944, as I sat at home after a day in the factory, I heard the familiar "clump" of the evening paper hitting the front door. When I went to pick it up, I saw a story that fired my imagination. Five missionaries had been killed by stone-age Indians in Bolivia. Then and there, I was challenged undeniably. Shaken to the core, I awakened to my responsibility. I knew what I must do with my life: I must follow in those men's footsteps, bring the Word of God to the peoples who had never heard of Jesus Christ. My hesitation and refusals were gone. I made my stand.

From then on my life took on one purpose: to follow those martyrs to Bolivia. But how to do it? I had no training in missionary work. But I determined that whatever was necessary I would somehow do.

And so it was that a few months after that memorable day, I enrolled in the missionary training course given in Chicago by the New Tribes Mission. There I received both physical and spiritual training. Intensive study of Scripture was combined with the wide variety of practical subjects in which a missionary must be versed— from boating to barbering, from farming to establishing an indigenous church. Following this, our class went to the Mendocino Forest in California, where we established a "missionary boot camp." Modeled after the military boot camps, this was the first of its kind. The objective was to simulate as closely as possible the conditions faced by missionaries in primitive areas, and hence to toughen them up as "commandos" for the Christian battlefield.

There our practical and spiritual learning was put to the test and driven home. There it was that we learned to trust to God in difficult situations. In the hard conditions imposed on us we were first able to comprehend the way God would miraculously meet our needs in time of adversity. Only after such rigorous physical stress, and such spiritual maturation, would we be able to endure the conditions of life beyond civilization, and allow God's way to work in us.

At Bible school in Chicago I had met Edith Olson, who was as zealous as I in her determination to carry the Word abroad. A few months later, in boot camp, we were married.

In the years that followed my challenge, my spiritual experience was deepened and broadened. I continued to study and work at both the Chicago school and the camp. Edith and I were blessed with two children, first Brian, then Connie. For two years, as we waited for the opportunity to go abroad, I worked as a tree surgeon in Marin County, California, at the same time directing a Youth-for-Christ movement there.

Then, at last, it was time to leave for Bolivia—the area where the missionaries who had challenged me in the first place lay down their lives.

In late September, 1949, the little missionary airplane took off from Corumba, a Brazilian town on the eastern border, and headed for war-torn Bolivia. My decision of nearly six years before was about to be consummated.

2

Facing the Unknown

From the air we saw a great semidesert ahead of us. On the near edge of it, amid a patchwork of jungle and barren land, we sighted Robore and the airstrip. Coming in low for a landing, we were startled to see that the airfield was covered with oil drums. Ben Weatherald, our missionary aviation pilot, zoomed the plane up again and radioed the field for instructions. The Bolivian officers aboard explained this was only a routine precaution to prevent the rebels from landing supplies, and while Ben circled the field, they identified themselves to the ground. Soon, tiny figures emerged and rolled the oil drums away.

The plane touched down smoothly and taxied to a stop in front of a low red-brick building. At last we were in Bolivia. We didn't know what lay ahead, but at least we had reached the country of our destination.

We piled out and stood breathing deeply of the hot, dry Bolivian air. We were glad to be on the ground again. The scene appeared peaceful enough; we looked in vain for any signs of revolution.

"Listen!" someone exclaimed. Everybody stood still. From the distance came the sound of another plane.

"The rebels!" said a man standing next to me in a hushed voice. People started running for cover. Men appeared from every direction, rolling out the barrels again. One of the army officers called out to us, "Get away from that plane—it's likely to be bombed!"

Edith and I grabbed the children and scurried for the comparative protection of a nearby building. We tried our best to appear calm, in order to avoid the barrage of questions Brian would pour forth.

Two planes swooped down, circled around without firing a shot, and veered away. Then they came back. I was sure they were going to let us have it this time. But they didn't. They swept round the field and disappeared once more—this time for good.

Feeling slightly weak in the knees, I started back to the plane to pick up our bags when I heard a voice cry, "Hi, you kids! Is it ever good to see you two!"

A slight brown-haired figure in a blue-print house dress was running toward us. I recognized Helen Ostewig. Helen had taken to calling us "You kids" ever since Brian was born. One night when she had come to visit us while we were all working together at mission headquarters, she had remarked that we looked like two kids playing with a live doll. Is there anything like the sight of a familiar, beloved face when you are a stranger in a foreign land? Considering the experience we had just been through, the sight of Helen was especially welcome. The kisses, hugs, and embraces that followed—the holding off for a second look!

Helen was a very special person in our lives. It was she—then secretary to Paul Fleming, director of our sponsoring organization, the New Tribes Mission—who had answered favorably my first letter of application. From the very beginning she had helped me in my missionary career. When Edith and I were living in Chicago, her warm and radiant personality led us to seek her friendship. Later, she married Jim Ostewig.

We had hoped for the possibility—which now seemed about to be realized—of working in pairs of couples in the same tribal area, according to the policy of our mission. In fact, we had planned to leave the States on the same plane with Jim and Helen. But a few days before, Edith and I had given up our space to Joy and Myron Gess, since Joy was in that part of her pregnancy during which it is safest to travel. So the Ostewigs had gone on ahead. We had hoped to meet them somewhere along the line, but with conditions as they were, we did not know where or when that might be.

Connie Wyma also made her way over to give us a hearty welcome. Both she and her husband, Mel, a missionary pilot, were old friends of ours, having started training at the same time we did.

"But where's Jim?" I asked at once.

"Oh, he's gone on ahead," Helen replied. "Come on, let's start walking. You'll have to carry your bags to the mission home. It's only about half a mile. I'll tell you all about it as we go." Conversation bubbled from her in a pent-up stream. "We've got our post," Helen said. "At least I *think* we have. Jim's up there right now."

"Mel flew him in," added Connie. "They left a few days ago."

"Oh, really?" asked Edith eagerly. "Where is it?"

"Sort of a backwoods settlement called Cafetal."

"Cafetal?" I said. "Never even heard of it."

Helen laughed. "You and a whole lot of other people. I've hardly found anyone who *has* heard of it. All I know is that it's somewhere up north in the jungle right smack on the border between Bolivia and Brazil." Her voice took on an eager tone. "I understand that there are a number of really primitive tribes to be reached from there. It's hard to believe, but they are savages living exactly the way they did thousands of years ago."

Edith murmured her surprise. She wanted to know how Jim and Helen came to decide on Cafetal.

"It's the strangest story," Helen continued. "Honestly—the people God finds way to use! Eight weeks or so ago, this man turned up here in Robore, an Austrian, tall, very erect—had 'army' written all over him. He had great continental charm, but there was something mysterious about him. He admitted he was an adventurer. He had been all over this country looking for gold. His name is Frederico.

"He has been living for some time in Cafetal. Jim and Mel promised him that if he would have an airstrip made, then our two families would go up there to work. He said he would do so. Last month Jim and Mel flew up there, saw that the strip was too short, and dropped a note for Frederico, asking him to lengthen it. Aside from that, there's nothing I can tell you about Cafetal—I don't know any more."

We had almost reached the home, where we were to stay for a few days. As all of us began to pour in, I thought the towns-people must have wondered how that small four-room house was going to contain a whole planeload of missionaries.

In the yard, Helen Ostewig paused. Laying a hand on my arm, she called my attention to a long, low building next door with whitewashed mud walls and a red-tiled roof. "Do you recognize that place?" she asked softly.

Tears came to my eyes. I could not speak. I could only nod dumbly. Did I know it! This was the house which had been head-quarters for the five missionaries who lost their lives trying to make contact with the Ayores. How many times had I seen it during my training course in the motion pictures the five had sent back to the States! To me it was a holy place. And here I was looking at it with my own eyes.

I let the others go on into the house. My mind was still full of the events of the past few days. First, my mother's tears and my fa-ther's strained composure during the painful farewells in front of their home in Lansing: they had not known when, if ever, they would see any of the four of us again, since we were venturing into one of the wildest areas on earth, where many had died before us. And the rude jolt our hopes had received at the Miami airport in the splashed headlines of the outbreak of revolution in Bolivia —which could mean the closing of all doors to our work there. Then the night spent curled up on the cold floor of a badly overcrowded Puerto Rican hotel. And the next night, in which our missionary plane had, for several terrifying minutes, been lost over northeastern Brazil as a result of a storm and a shorted-out radio—until, with the Lord's help, our pilot, Ben Weatherald, finally found the city of Belem and landed safely. Brian, four, and Connie, a year old, had slept peacefully through it all.

Then the headlines there—

BOLIVIAN PRESIDENT HANGED FROM LAMPPOST

—bringing new fears, making us wonder whether it was worthwhile to go on. More travel. Then the fortune of finding some Bolivian army officers who would help us get into the country in trade for our giving them a plane lift.

I looked again at the house of the five missionaries. As I gazed on it, from deep within me there was gathered a new strength, a new determination. At that spot I prayed with the thought of those men in my mind, to help me in the Lord's unfinished work that lay ahead.

Inside, the pleasant little living room of the missionary home resembled a refugee center, with suitcases and duffel bags piled all over the place. But this didn't bother anyone. Helen and Connie Wyma fell to and soon had a good supper of Spanish rice and green salad ready.

Under the impact of our new experiences, we had forgotten about the revolution. But as night fell there came a grim reminder of the proximity of the rebel forces: the counting off of the guards. "*Uno—dos—tres,*" they barked. Having little hope of being able to sleep, we tucked the children away early under their mosquito nets and, with cups of strong Bolivian coffee balanced on our knees, sat down to talk.

Mel and Connie Wyma had been in the field in Bolivia for three years. Mel, who had flown his Stinson down from the States himself, had made some contacts with the Ayores. I thought Connie might be able to tell me some things I did not know about the fate of the five missionaries they had killed.

"None of us has been able to learn enough of the Ayore language or make friendly enough contact with all of them to shed any more light on what really happened," Connie said. "At first everybody assumed they'd all been killed. But the widows held out hope there was still a possibility—slight though it was—that they might be alive somewhere off there in the jungle. Finally, though, someone was able to speak with the killers themselves—their death is confirmed."

A shot rang out. We jumped. Helen acted as though this were nothing unusual. But the conversation turned to the chances of fighting breaking out again.

Connie's remarks had renewed my missionary ardor. Perhaps my work would lead me to find out more about the men. I would then be fulfilling the dedication I had made to follow in their footsteps, if the Lord should lead in that direction.

Later that evening two of the widows came over to call. In perfect calm, they told of the events leading up to and following the tragedy—of their hopes and their faith. It was one of the most moving experiences in my life.

Someone suggested we get to bed. Around midnight Connie Wyma showed me the quarters they had arranged for the men, which consisted of a palm-leaf-thatched shack thirty yards behind the house. A few nationals had been hired to erect the shelter in anticipation of our arrival. Five or six jungle hammocks were strung under the roof for us. One by one, we crawled into them. We were exhausted. No one spoke. The night was heavy with warm air. There was only the furious croaking of the frogs, as if each were trying to outdo the other. Now and again, when they would all suddenly stop, we would wonder whether someone were intruding into their territory. My eyes were heavy, though, and I sank into the first light waves of sleep.

Suddenly there was a burst of gunfire. Bullets were whining through the air over our heads. We tumbled out of our hammocks as fast as we could untangle ourselves. We hurried into the house to see if our wives and children were all right. They were, although some of the children were awake and crying with fear. We ourselves badly needed reassurrance, but we tried to quiet them. Then, as quickly as it had begun, the shooting stopped.

After a silence, the counting off of the guards started once more. We listened tensely.

"Uno—dos—"

A sniper's bullet had silenced number three. Our hearts went out to the poor fellow; we wondered how badly he had been hurt. Before long a new voice answered for number three. The air continued to echo their calls.

But the frogs remained silent. From this I inferred that the rebels must still be stalking around. Sure enough, an hour or so later the rifles barked out again. This time the bullets seemed even closer to the house. Another countdown. No response from number five. One by one, lives were being snuffed out.

After they had been held awhile, the children grew calm and went back to bed. It was almost morning. We returned to our hammocks.

With the dawn of our second day in Robore came a good deal of discussion about what had gone on during the night. As Connie Wyma opened up the wooden shutters, the orange light of the rising sun burst into the dark living room.

"Well," Connie half yawned, "did you kids get any sleep last night?"

"Sleep, what's that?" I said. I was behind Edith with my arms around her.

"Wow!" Edith exclaimed. "When the shooting began, I thought I'd jump out of my skin."

Soon the good smell of oatmeal cooking on the wood stove brought a feeling of home.

"I wonder who's in charge of the government this morning?" I asked, as I walked over to look out of the open top half of the door.

Outside, everything looked calm. A few women in clean but faded, shapeless dresses drifted by, carrying a handful of vegetables or hunks of meat. Most went barefoot, with their long black hair streaming down their backs. Looking down the sandy street at the row of houses, I saw dust flying out the doors as the brick floors were swept. Smoke rose slowly into the sky from open fires.

"Eeeek!" one of the women squealed from behind me. "There's a scorpion!"

Connie Wyma walked over and casually stepped on it.

"You'll get used to them," she said. "They're all over the place. Some days we kill half a dozen of them."

With forty-eight hours' layover, Edith and I had a chance to stroll through the town with the youngsters. It didn't take us long the first day to realize we were the objects of special curiosity. Every time one of us paused to look behind us, or turned our heads in an unexpected direction, a fleeting figure would vanish into a doorway, or a head would pop out of a window and back. This seemed strange, since we were certainly not the first Americans they had seen. But we didn't think too much about it.

Early the next day two or three women came to the door to sell some bananas, rice bread, or corn biscuits. Naturally they wanted the pleasure of telling anything that was new. Their word that morning was that the government forces had recaptured Cochabamba (the provincial capital and hopefully our destination).

A few minutes later an army general arrived to beg us to fly him and other officers to Cochabamba. He assured us he would provide all help possible with the officials when we got there. He warned us, however, that the plane might be shot at on the way, since commercial and private planes had been forbidden to fly during the revolution. None of the party enjoyed the prospect. Ben pointed out, however, that if we didn't go, there was no telling when we might get to Cochabamba. This proved the decisive argument.

The same afternoon, we men took the children swimming at a delightful, concealed spot in a creek half a mile from the house. When we returned, Ben was laughing heartily.

"You'll never believe it, Bruce," he said. "I found out why you were such objects of curiosity. One of the missionary kids said they heard the discussion in school and let me in on it. Padre Juan told all the kids in town you were devils! They were looking for your tails!"

Offended, Brian said indignantly, "I don't have a tail." We all laughed.

"But they know the truth now," Ben said. "One of the kids followed you out to the swimming hole to see for sure, and now the word is out that the priest was wrong—no tails, no devils!"

Next morning, as we trundled out to the airport, there were few words among us. Each was lost in his private thoughts. The officers from the barracks talked over the flight with Ben, as Helen translated. Ben seemed reluctant to take the chance. He was not so concerned over his own safety as he was over the lives of the missionary families. When we made it clear we were willing to take the chance and even anxious to go, he consented. The order went out for the barrels to be rolled away.

Our destination, the city of Cochabamba, where our mission had its headquarters, lay tucked in a fertile Andean valley eight thousand feet high, about four hundred and fifty miles away. We would have to cross very high mountains, and then, upon approaching the town, dive in and land as quickly as possible to avoid being shot down. In view of the situation, the officers did not want to advise the airfield in advance of our arrival. The plane leveled off at eighteen thousand feet, with the tops of the jagged peaks some two thousand feet below.

We slipped through a high pass and the plane began to lose altitude rapidly. Our Connie began to cry: she couldn't get her eardrums to pop. Others were yawning hard or pushing on their ears. I waited for the first sound of gunfire. Seconds, minutes, ticked by. Was the decision made back in Robore, not to radio ahead, the correct one? The officers had reasoned it would deny the ground officials the opportunity of refusing us entrance. But didn't it make us all the more likely to look like a rebel plane? We were dropping, dropping, every second bringing us closer. Suddenly we were on the runway, a smooth landing.

Everyone sighed and began to talk rapidly—except our young Connie, who, startled by the noise and still having trouble with her ears, began to cry louder than ever. Edith took her in her arms and sat in the seat Connie had been occupying and comforted her.

We taxied to a stop at the end of the airport farthest from the buildings and conning tower. Many of the smaller children were crying. Their mothers kept trying to get them to yawn or to hold their noses and blow, to make their ears pop.

A jeep, loaded with heavily-armed soldiers, raced toward us. Four of the soldiers leaped out and ran to the plane. Ben opened the door and they came aboard, keeping their bayoneted rifles pointed at him and at us. The officers with us explained who we were and why we had come. Satisfied that we were not prepared to do battle with them, their commander ordered some of them back to the jeep and commanded Ben to taxi behind the jeep, which he did. They led us to the front of an army barracks and stopped. Out of the building poured at least a hundred soldiers in battle dress, the muzzles of their bayoneted rifles pointed squarely at the plane. Half a dozen fighter planes were lined up behind the spot where the soldiers took up their positions on the runway. Looking over the shining bayonets and helmets, I watched one soldier climb into the cockpit of a plane. The black barrel of a machine gun protruded from the nose, directly toward us, and I tried to calculate the probable path of the bullets if the man accidentally pushed the wrong button. They would go just about—

Rat-a-tat-tat-tat! the gun barked. Everyone jumped, even the soldiers. The bullets seared the air over the plane, then stopped abruptly. We wondered whether it had been a mistake or a deliberate attempt to frighten us.

At last the officers who had accompanied us climbed out of the plane and explained again who we were and what we were doing here. After much talk, the majority of the troops were ordered back to the barracks. The tension was beginning to wear us down. We men stood in a huddle, talking about the red tape. Finally, after about an hour of waiting, Ben and Helen, who had been talking with the officials, came to explain that the latter were still very suspicious and angry at the way we had come in, but were more or less convinced we meant no harm. We could go now.

A cordon of soldiers herded us into the back of a truck. They climbed in after us, their bayonets still fixed, their expressions hostile. The truck pulled out. Helen explained we were being taken to the mission headquarters at long last. We rumbled along through the middle of the city. People looked at us, no doubt wondering where the soldiers were taking the truckload of foreigners.

We passed by the Plaza, in the main part of Cochabamba. Everywhere were the scars of war—broken windows, once-stately palm trees shattered by shellfire, adobe walls pockmarked with bullet holes. Soldiers still patrolled the streets. But all was quiet now—the city was once again firmly under government control.

We were glad to find ourselves behind the six-foot wall surrounding the mission headquarters. It was like coming home. The yard was well landscaped and green with shrubbery, the sort of patio one might find in California or Florida. Inside, the house had a pleasant sort of Spanish style, with wide glass windows, cream-colored walls, tile floors, and upholstered furniture.

Myron and Joy Gess, the missionaries in charge, who had taken our place on the first flight from the States over two months before we left, were there to welcome us. They had their hands full, rearranging sleeping and eating accommodations for the influx of new guests. About half of our original planeload of missionaries had come on with us to Cochabamba; the others had remained in Robore.

Helen immediately asked Joy if there were any letters for her. No—there were none. Helen had hoped to find a note from Jim. She tried to conceal her disappointment by helping Joy get the dinner ready.

The tide of the revolution had turned in favor of the government. Each day the newspapers brought stories of the arrest of more rebels. We were glad to be left free and alone.

In our naïveté about the Latin notion of time, we had expected our household goods, which had been shipped by sea six months before our departure, would be ready and waiting for us. But the cargo of trunks and boxes, we learned, had yet to be unloaded at Antofagasta, Chile, from where they would have to be transferred to one of the puffing, snorting trains on the narrow-gauge railway that threads its way up over the Andes to Cochabamba. Days passed with no sign of our shipment. All our inquiries were greeted with shrugs and the polite, vague phrases of bureaucracy.

Also, nothing had been heard from Jim. Helen was growing more and more uneasy. A letter had come from Connie Wyma, saying that Mel Wyma left Jim in good shape at the airstrip and had gone off to fly some supplies to missionaries working with the Ayores. After that—for weeks—Helen had heard nothing.

I now thought it would be a good idea to find out what I could about Cafetal, if only to reassure Helen. I went to call on a few merchants in town first, for I had heard that traders from that area, which was more than a thousand miles away, sometimes came to Cochabamba to sell their alligator and jaguar hides and snakeskins. What they told me was hardly reassuring. Cafetal had come into existence only about fifty years before as an army outpost. But the entire garrison, including the colonel, had been wiped out by malaria. For a number of years it had remained uninhabited. Then a small settlement of rubber workers had grown up there, partly because it was on the Rio Guaporé and hence accessible to supplies by the mail boat, which ran twice a month. Cafetal was still looked upon as one of the worst pest holes in all Bolivia, so far as malaria was concerned. I thought confidently of our supplies of Paludrine (malaria preventative) that we purchased in Cochabamba. If malaria were all we had to worry about! (I had to be careful how much depressing information I passed on to Helen and Edith.)

The unexpectedly long duration of our stay in Cochabamba brought a financial pinch. With the end of our first week, in fact, came the end of our money. The delays en route, the hotel and restaurant bills, had already melted away most of what we had counted on to tide us over. A month before, we had received about a thousand dollars for our needs. But most of that had gone at once for plane fare. Our friends at home had no means of knowing of our plight. Help seemed very far away right now.

One night, after the children were tucked in bed, Edith and I sat down to talk things over. Payment had been due that day for our next week's board at the mission home. We could have asked for credit, of course, but it had been a long-standing principle of ours never to do so. As it was, we would have to defer payment for that evening at least. We tried to take our minds off our problems by walking around town to absorb what we could of Bolivian life. Cochabamba, a city of a hundred thousand, is about equally divided between persons of Spanish descent and Quechua (pronounced *catch-u-ah*) Indians. These Indians, as workers or slaves, had made up a large percentage of the Inca empire hundreds of years ago. The Spanish people are the descendants of the Conquistadors who went to South America and destroyed the Inca rule and empire. Many Quechuas still live in much the same primitive way as their ancestors did under the old civilization. Many others have entered into the democratic, commercial way of modern Bolivian life.

Most of the buildings are built perilously close to the street. Frequently, the sidewalk narrows to about a foot in width. If a person happens to be walking in such a spot when a truck roars by, he is well advised to step hastily into a doorway or at least pull in his stomach, if he doesn't wish to lose a few buttons from his shirt.

Since it is hard for drivers to see around street corners, they rely on their horns to let others know they are coming. The din is terrific. Traffic regulations must be very lax, for everyone drives like a madman. The cars show the scars of the battle, too: one seldom sees fenders not banged up or ripped off.

In the Cochabamba marketplace, the hefty Quechua women wear bright-colored skirts containing, Edith estimated, about three yards of material more than necessary; full, half-sleeved blouses adorned with yards of lace; and hard, white, derbylike hats.

Courtesy is hardly the byword. These women plow through a crowd like a fullback hitting the line, and woe to any skinny American like me who happens to get in their way! Whether going to shop or to work, they carry for miles huge bundles on their backs. They sit with vegetables, fruit, clothing, and other odds and ends spread around them, paying no attention whatever to the millions of flies feasting on the food.

With time on my hands, I was growing restless. I volunteered to help Myron crate up supplies to be sent to the missionaries scattered around Bolivia. As I nailed up crates and wrapped packages destined for the use of others, I had a hard time suppressing my temptation to envy, wishing those supplies were for us. Every few days, I made the trip to the *aduana* (customs house), asked the same question, and received the same answer: "Nothing today, *señor*."

Once, upon returning from one of these futile excursions, I found a note from Lyle Sharp, a missionary friend from the States. Lyle was stationed at Guajara Mirim, a frontier town five hundred miles over the mountains from Cochabamba.

I opened the note eagerly: "I find that a boat leaves Guajara Mirim for Cafetal November 5," Lyle had written. "I hope you will all be on it. Why don't you get here a few days early so we can have a good visit before you leave?" The fifth and twenty-fifth of every month a government mail boat left Guajara Mirim for Cafetal, five hundred miles up the Rio Guaporé. But I almost had to laugh. Didn't we wish we could? It was now the latter part of October. We had been in Cochabamba since mid-September. Friends informed us it might be months before our household goods arrived. This, too, was a part of pioneer missionary life we had not foreseen—the waiting, the endless waiting.

I tried to tell myself it was no use worrying about Jim, out there alone in the wilderness. But I couldn't seem to help it. Suppose he needed us desperately? Why hadn't he written? And here we sat.

It was made no easier by the shaky state of our finances. Every few days we would get down to our last cent as we exhausted the money sent to us by friends and supporters in the States. Three square meals a day were being served at the mission home table, but we had decided not to partake unless we could pay. When we found ourselves in these situations, I drew comfort from reading Matthew 6:26: "Behold the fowls of the air: for they sow not, neither do they reap, nor gather into barns; yet your heavenly Father feedeth them. Are ye not much better than they?" And time after time our need was met—five dollars, fifteen dollars, three dollars—always enough to keep us going.

One day, as I was mentally counting up our meager resources, I noticed Helen Ostewig staring off into space. Lyle's letter was in her hand. "You know, I've been thinking," she said slowly. "I believe I'd better go ahead and fly to Guajara Mirim to catch the November fifth boat to Cafetal, without waiting for you. You can come later as soon as our shipments arrive. Still nothing from Jim. Mel is off in the jungle somewhere—he can't fly me in. Somehow I can't bear the thought of waiting here another month for the December fifth boat."

Day after day we had watched Helen's strain increasing. Normally a calm, placid person, she was getting nervous. We could only agree that her decision was the wise one. A few days later we saw her off at the airport. When it came time for her to go, Edith kissed her good-by and I took her hand and said cheerfully, "We'll see you next month in Cafetal." As the plane became a tiny speck in the distance, I said, "The Lord bless you and keep you."

More days and weeks went by. The checks were coming more often now, so that our financial strain was somewhat eased in the sense that the periods between penniless days grew longer. Then, one day shortly after the middle of November, the morning mail brought a formal notice from the *aduana*. Our household goods had reached Cochabamba and so had Helen and Jim's. Now we could go. And we might even have time to catch the December 5 boat.

Crates and boxes arrived at the missionary home. Hurriedly, Edith and I started checking things over and repacking. Edith had fun making lists for our food supplies. We had to keep reminding ourselves that we were buying for three months—not merely a week or two. Oh, the number of items we planned to lay in—rice, flour, salt, sugar, canned meat and vegetables, dried apples and peaches, raisins, oatmeal, lard, dried soup, tomato paste, bacon, spices, and so on!

Then our house of dreams came tumbling down—when we went out to the airport and found what the freight charges to Guajara Mirim would be. They came to more money than we had, quite aside from leaving enough to buy additional needed supplies. Edith and I returned to the house. Our friends, who had rejoiced with us in the arrival of our household goods, wondered at our serious faces and forced smiles. We told them of our disappointment. All we could do was wait for funds from the States. But for how many more weeks, months? Our faith was sorely tried.

A day or two later, one of our fellow missionaries dropped in to talk about things in general. Then he fell silent and sat for a moment with his chin cupped in his hands. He seemed to be undergoing some kind of inner struggle. Then he stood up and came over to me. "The Lord spoke to my heart about a need you may have," he said, and pressed upon me ten thousand Bolivianos (about a hundred dollars). He left as soon as I had thanked him, and I was glad he did—because I could hardly speak, for I knew what his spontaneous generosity must have meant to him. He had denied himself to give to us. He would forego some luxury—even some necessity—to meet our need.

I embraced Edith. Then we went off with high hearts to revel in buying supplies.

3

On the Edge of Darkness

We mounted the steps of the two-engine commercial plane at the airport in Cochabamba and waved good-by to the missionaries who had come to see us off. (At least we tried our best to wave, loaded down as we were with all our gear!) A thrill of anticipation went through me as I fastened my seat belt and heard the engines kick over and roar to life.

A long trip lay ahead: five hundred miles by plane, five hundred more by river boat. At the end we would find a change in our way of life more extreme than any we had undergone before. I knew it would be especially trying for Edith—cooking over an open fire, washing clothes in the river, sweeping a hard-packed mud floor were only a few of the inconveniences we might face. But she seemed to welcome the prospect.

Her background had been a hard one, and she was well suited to be a missionary wife. As a young girl, growing up on a small farm in northern Wisconsin, she had been entrusted with most of the responsibility for her younger brothers and sisters. I glanced at the woman sitting next to me and remembered the girl I had begun to notice at the night Bible and missionary training classes in Chicago, a girl with that same reddish-brown hair and smiling, freckled face. I remembered the long walks we had begun taking and the endless talks of our hopes and dreams. Our interests in missionary work that had sprouted and grown together were finally entwined as we joined our lives. Today, these interests, which had become one, were reaching fruition. We were going to the field to take up the work to which we had been called.

Edith seemed to be reading my thoughts, for she squeezed my hand and said, "Think of the opportunities that lie ahead for us. Isn't it wonderful to be here?"

Six hours after leaving Cochabamba we put down at Guayara-merin, the Bolivian airport town across the river from Guajara Mirim, Brazil. We were in the lowlands; after that high altitude, getting out of the plane was like stepping into a steam room.

"Let's go back to Cochabamba, Dad," said Brian in disgust. "It's hot down here."

"You'll get used to it, son," I replied. "Here—take your sweater off. Maybe that'll help."

Edith was already peeling layers of blanket from Connie.

"Sort of like Chicago on a summer afternoon, only worse," she remarked.

Lyle Sharp met us. "It sure is great to see you," he said, shaking our hands warmly. "It isn't very often we get folks from home out this way!"

It was a comfort to see Lyle's friendly face out here in this steaming, lonely, unfamiliar spot. A heavy-set man then in his late thirties, he was slow in his movements and deliberate in his speech, undoubtedly owing to his boyhood on a small Midwestern farm, which made it easy for him to adapt to the leisurely pace of Latin-American life. His ready smile which crinkled up in little crow's feet around his blue eyes, and his air of quiet confidence made you feel that when you were with Lyle he had your welfare at heart and you were in good hands.

"I guess Helen got off all right?" Edith asked.

"Oh, yes," said Lyle a bit hastily. "She caught the November 5 government boat to Cafetal as planned. Come—I'll help you get your bags down to the river. We have to cross in a dugout. Guajara Mirim, where we live, is on the Brazilian side." I thought I noticed some constraint in Lyle's normally outgoing, easy manner. Why did he steer the conversation away from Helen so quickly?

The youngsters got a big kick out of crossing in the dugout, which was driven by a powerful outboard. Edith and I didn't enjoy it so much, for the boat was tippy and close to the waterline.

The route to the Sharps' house took us through the town. Guajara Mirim was picturesque—at least one could say that for it. It reminded me of the sort of frontier towns seen in westerns. The first thing to catch my eye were hundreds of rolls of brown crude rubber. They filled the air with the odor of smoky bacon. Nearby were stacked mounds of dark brown, moonshaped Brazil nuts. Before the open-front stores hung alligator and jaguar hides, and, now and then, the skin of a huge anaconda.

A shrill, piping whistle startled us. We turned and saw by the railroad station an old relic of an engine. It wheezed as though it had a bad case of asthma. "Quite a story behind that railroad," said Lyle as we walked. "A few years ago some company started to build a railroad for two hundred miles downriver to Porto Velho —oceangoing ships come that far up the Amazon. The way lay through steaming jungles. One company after another gave up. Indians attacked many of the workers. It was even thought the Indians poisoned the water, because the men died like flies—but nobody knows whether that's true or not. Anyway, after many tries, the railroad finally got built. But what a staggering price for it in lives and money! They say approximately one man died for every tie on the railroad. It's hard to believe, but it must have cost two hundred thousand lives, to build two hundred miles of railroad. And look at it now."

Awed by the story he had just told us, we were quiet.

Lila Sharp and the two boys were waiting at the house gate to greet us. She was the same gay, slender, vital Lila we remembered from training days. She had a room ready for us and made us feel right at home. After supper, with the children put to bed, we sat on the porch talking, just as we might have done back home.

"Now tell us about Helen," Edith asked once more.

Lyle seemed not to hear her. "Do you know anything of the history of this town?" he asked. And he was off on another of his stories. "During World War II, when rubber was in short supply and needed desperately for our war effort, men were sent to this area to look for wild rubber. Many were brought in by hydroplane —a lot of them right around here. Airplanes would land on the rivers at appointed times to pick up the rubber. But often as not they'd find no one to meet them—the men had died somewhere off in the jungle. They say out of the twenty-five thousand or so, only maybe seven thousand came out alive. Anyway, Guajara Mirim became kind of a rubber depot then—and it's remained one ever since. You wouldn't imagine how close the thick jungle comes up to the edge of town. Even today, men from the wild Pacaas Novos tribe come up at night and kill a cow or two, or sometimes some people."

The thought made us shudder. We wondered if Cafetal would be this wild or even wilder. Edith tried to steer the conversation back to Helen, but just then a loud roll of thunder arrested our attention.

"Sounds like we're in for a good one tonight," said Lyle. We jumped up and began to close the shutters to keep the rain from pouring in.

Before long the storm broke—a real tropical downpour. It was almost as though the elements were putting on a demonstration for our benefit. The wind roared; the rain came down in buckets. We could talk no longer above the noise. So we went to bed.

At dawn, cats, dogs, and roosters awakened us. I wandered around the house. Lila was already busy preparing oatmeal and coffee. Edith got the children dressed and fed the baby.

"Where's Lyle?" I asked Lila, thinking he might at least tell me something about Helen if I met him alone.

Lila looked at her watch and replied, "Oh, he should be here any minute. He has to get up at four o'clock every morning to go to the market."

"Four o'clock!"

"Yes, if he's late the meat and the few vegetables that might be on the stands are gone."

"Wouldn't it be nice to have a refrigerator," I said, "so that you could buy a big hunk of meat at a time?"

Lila smiled.

"Oh, we're getting used to doing without such things."

Lyle came in and we had breakfast. Before we had finished he went to his room and returned with his Bible.

"Here, Bruce," he said. "Why don't you read the Ninety-first Psalm?"

I read that beautiful passage which ends with: ". . . Thou shalt not be afraid for the terror by night; nor for the arrow that flieth by day; nor for the pestilence that walketh in darkness; nor for the destruction that walketh at noonday. . . . For he shall give his angels charge over thee, to keep thee in all thy ways."

I wondered why he had chosen this selection for me to read at this particular time. Was he trying to prepare me for something?

We let the children finish their prayers so they could go play in the fenced-in backyard. Soon Brian and the Sharp boys were making roads in the sandy soil and pulling their trucks around. Connie was still little enough to be a nuisance, and we could hear the boys yelling at her to get out of the way.

The rest of us lingered around the table. It was the missionary hour of prayer and meditation.

"I think we should pray especially this morning for the safety of Helen and Jim," began Lyle. He was very serious.

"Poor Helen," he said, looking up. "We both felt so sorry for her. She had such a hard time making up her mind."

"About what?" I asked.

"About whether she should take the November fifth boat or stay and wait for you."

"But that was all settled before she left Cochabamba," said Edith in surprise.

"Yes, but at that time she hadn't heard the rumors."

"What rumors?" I demanded.

"That Jim was dead."

"Jim—dead?"

The words stunned me.

"Of course we haven't the slightest idea there's any truth in them," Lyle added quickly. "I guess we're more used to hearing rumors in this part of the world than you are."

"How did you hear them?" I asked.

"It was after a commercial boat came in. People stopped me on the street and asked if I knew the American who had been killed in Cafetal. Only one thing in all the stories was the same—the man had been found on the banks of the Guaporé shot by the Indians. I did not know of any American in Cafetal except Jim. I hated to tell Helen. But I felt I had to; she was getting ready to leave.

"I will never forget her look. Her mouth dropped. Her eyes widened. Her breath came in short gasps. All she said was, 'I don't know what to do.' Then she turned to us. 'What should I do?' she asked.

"I didn't know what to say to her. She looked at it this way and that. She said, 'If anything *has* happened there seems to be no point in my going upriver by myself. I'll be all alone—no friends—nothing I can do. No one to turn to who could help me or comfort me. Yet, if I don't go, Jim might worry about me. Or what if he's been hurt and needs me? I'd never forgive myself.'

"She talked like this very often for the next few days until it was nearly time for the boat to leave. Then one morning she said, 'I've made up my mind. I'm going upriver to Jim—even though I have to go alone. Ask Edith and Bruce to come as soon as they can. I'll need them.'

"I longed to accompany her. But Lila could not go—she had no one with whom to leave the children. And for a male missionary to be traveling alone with the wife of another missionary could start talk—Latins look at those things differently than we do. So, reluctantly we had to let her go alone. Helen insisted she'd be all right, even though she was the only woman on the boat. It was with heavy hearts that we went down to see her off."

We spent a few moments praying for Jim and Helen, then Lila and Edith cleared off the table and began to do the dishes.

"I'm glad we don't have long to wait before the next boat," Edith said. "Oh, how terrible to be without any communication when you want so much to know."

Little else was said. Lila and Edith were feeling with Helen the inner struggle a woman goes through in such a situation. It hurt them as much as though Lyle or I had been the subject of the rumors.

Only a few more days remained, but the hours dragged. We could hardly wait to get started on our river trip to Cafetal.

Yet our hearts were filled with misgivings. Jim Ostewig was one of my buddies; we had been through rugged bootcamp training days in California together. We were counting on Helen and Jim's fellowship to help us through the first hard days of adjusting to life on the frontier. We had been looking forward to our meeting with Jim. But we had missed him at Robore. He had not showed up in Cochabamba—in fact, nothing had been heard from him. Now we had to face the possibility that we might never see him again on this earth. But if tragedy had occurred, then Helen would be needing us and we must get to her without delay.

4

Reconnaissance

We were glad when word went through Guajara Mirim that our boat was ready to leave. Only when we reached Cafetal would we know whether Jim were still alive and how Helen was faring.

The great storm a few nights before had ushered in the rainy season. Our spirits rose when Lyle told us that since the Rio Guaporé was at high water, the boat trip would take only about eight days instead of the usual fifteen.

Weighted down with our hand luggage, and accompanied by helpful Brazilians who carried our household goods, Edith, Connie, Brian, and I joined the handful of Portuguese-speaking families heading toward the wharf. At the last minute, Lyle decided to go to Cafetal to help us on the way with language and any other problems, then return on the same boat. Lila and the two boys came to see us off.

My head was filled with romantic notions about that riverboat. I had pictured, perhaps from reading Mark Twain, a big, double-decked paddle-wheeler with plush staterooms, all gilt-and-white paint and shining brass.

As we approached the wharf, I had my first hint of rude reality.

On either side of the path, thrusting up from the weeds and the grass like the skeletons of prehistoric monsters, were the rotting ribs of old abandoned river craft. We reached the water's edge.

"Where's the mail boat?" I asked, thinking perhaps it had not come in yet.

"Right there in front of you," said Lyle with a laugh.

I had mistaken the boat in front of us for some kind of floating store. It was about thirty feet long, I estimated, and perhaps ten feet wide. It was already loaded down with assorted cargo—sacks of salt, sugar, and rice; square tins of gasoline and kerosene; and stinking bundles of salted, dried meat. The weight of the cargo pushed the gunwales down to within about a foot of the water. I noticed the crust of white crystals caking the ribs of the hull. Perhaps, I thought, this might at least give some protection against the dry rot that had brought so many boats to the graveyard on the bank. We all went on board.

"But where's the place for the passengers?" I asked. I saw no deck—only a kind of catwalk about a foot wide running around the outside.

"We just string our hammocks between those posts," said Lyle. "Otherwise we sit on the rice or bean sacks." I guessed there was space for about ten hammocks. (I didn't know then that as we stopped to pick up passengers along the way, there would be as many as thirty of us.)

Overhead a palm-leafed canopy would give protection against the sun and somewhat against tropical downpours. I was surprised the ship had no engine. Then I saw the source of motive power—a long steel hull with a diesel engine in it lashed to one side. A man I took to be the pilot was bent over it, spinning the flywheel. The motor sputtered and coughed. As the hands began untying the mooring ropes, Lila and the boys trundled ashore and stood ready to wave to us from the bank.

The captain came up, introduced himself, and helped us find places for our hammocks. He wore no uniform, not even a visored cap—only an old khaki shirt and trousers. He appeared to be more a social director than a captain. (The real responsibility, I was to learn, lay with the pilot. His was a tricky job. It took a lot of skill to maneuver that sluggish craft around sunken logs and rocks, and over sandbars.)

Edith, with a woman's practicality, went off around the boat to locate the essentials for living: the kitchen, and some place where we might take a bath, change clothes, and wash Connie's diapers. It didn't take her long to find them. The kitchen, or galley, was no more than a small, smoke-blackened space in the bow, protected against the wind on two sides by a board wall. There, a bearded German cook was trying to start a fire in a small, iron, wood-burning stove. At the stern she found a shack which was both bathroom and dressing room.

A bell clanged; a muscular brown arm spun the diesel flywheel. The engine began a rhythmical *thump-thump-thump* (a sound which was never to leave us, day or night). The lines were cast off; we hardly appeared to be making any headway against the swift, chocolate-brown current.

But we were moving; our journey into the unknown had begun.

The sun grew heavy in the west, slowly turning the gray haze over the river to orange, and making the jungle green seem all the greener, the more strange, the more mysterious and exotic. The pilot, in the steel diesel boat, hugged the shore so closely that we passengers, in the flat-bottomed wooden mail boat, were brushed occasionally by overhanging branches.

We were making, the pilot told us, no more than two miles an hour. Since the tropic twilight would be short-lived, we made ourselves ready for the night. We were soon enveloped in smoke as the cook stoked up the fire to prepare our supper. This smoke was to be with us for most of the trip, stinging our eyes so badly it was difficult to read or study. About seven o'clock, we were each handed a plate and a spoon in our hammocks. We ate the rice and beans all right, for we were hungry. But we could not stomach the meat (known locally as "sharky," for its taste).

We hardly slept that night; only a few feet away was the banging diesel, and we had to get used to the noise as well as the vibration of the boat.

Everything, however, was so new and exciting that we soon forgot our discomforts. Bright-colored parrots and toucans squawked their indignation at our invasion of their privacy. We kept our eyes fixed on the jungles along the bank for the sight of a monkey, a tapir, or a jaguar (which the nationals referred to as the *tigre*), but we saw none. The river itself had its own wonders. One morning, upon hearing the shout of a fellow passenger, we looked over the stern at a school of porpoises, each about five or six feet in length, following in our wake. They described silver arcs in the air as they playfully surfaced to blow out air through the trap doors in their heads and take in a fresh supply. We had never dreamed we would find porpoises up here, twenty-five hundred miles from the sea.

Whenever we stopped, some of the men would fish for pirhanas. About the size of sunfish, they travel in large schools. Brian's eyes widened when the men showed him their vicious, sawlike teeth, which could strip the flesh off a man in minutes. His eyes bulged even more when they told him of the electric eels—the deadly sting rays that lurked in those same waters—or when they pointed out three bumps resembling a floating log, but which were actually the nose and eyes of a surfacing alligator.

Meanwhile, Edith washed diapers. When she strung them out to dry along the line at the side, the boat took on a homey touch.

After each intriguing day, as night fell, the scents and fragrance of the jungle enveloped us. It was like traveling through the freshness of the countryside after a nice rain. With the children tucked safely into their hammocks for the night, Edith, Lyle, and I would sit on the rice sacks and gaze out into the inky blackness, wondering what the Lord had in store.

A palm tree, etched black against the moonlit sky, lent an aura of romance. I longed then to kiss my wife, but I dared not. We were surrounded with people of another country, and as missionaries we had to be on our best behavior.

But we felt something sinister in the unfathomable blackness, too. We knew that death lurked there—in many forms. The powers of darkness, against which we were committed to do battle, were almost palpable.

Edith and I spent a lot of our time with our noses in our Spanish grammars, trying to learn as much as we could of the language before we reached Cafetal.

One afternoon I was standing with some fellow passengers at the rail when I thought I heard the words *"gringo"* (foreigner); *"salvajes"* (savages); and *"han matado"* (have killed). I called to Lyle who spoke both Spanish and Portuguese, told him of what I had overheard, and asked him to see if he could learn more of what was being said.

He came back in a few minutes. Yes, the rumors of the death of a white missionary were on the boat too, although they added nothing to what he had heard in Guajara Mirim.

I had a cold feeling at the pit of my stomach. If the rumor should prove true, would it be wise—or even possible—for us to stay on by ourselves in Cafetal? Was our work for the Lord to receive a setback before it had even begun?

To keep from being overwhelmed by morbid thoughts, I turned to watching the river for sting rays and pirhanas.

About the third day out, when the unremitting diet of flavorless rice and beans was beginning to pall on us, a crewman informed us we were stopping at a settlement to butcher a cow. The prospect of fresh meat made our mouths water. And for the next couple of days we enjoyed the luxury of fresh broiled meat with every meal. Then we noticed that the carcass was kept hanging from a pole. Since the boat had no refrigeration and the heat of the tropics was intense, we wondered what would be done to keep it from spoiling.

It didn't take us long to find out. The meat was soon crawling with maggots. We thought the cook would throw it away. Not at all! We saw him slice off several steaks, throw them in the frying pan, carefully scrape off the maggots, pepper the meat a bit, and serve the steaks to us with the rice and beans. By now it was smelling just like the slabs of dried meat stacked near us. That was enough; no more "fresh" meat for this voyage. Edith said she could hardly wait for the day to do her own cooking again.

On the morning of the eighth day, the pilot shouted in Portuguese from the diesel (Lyle interpreted for us): "We'll reach Cafetal before night."

But the hours dragged; the boat seemed to crawl. This was without doubt the longest day of our trip. I could not concentrate on reading or studying. I no longer had any interest in scanning the riverbank. Edith and I sat in our hammocks, asking ourselves the same question over and over again: "Will we find Jim alive?"

Even the children, catching our feeling of anxiety, were restless and hard to keep occupied. I tried to break the monotony of waiting by taking a shower. This involved going into the tiny cubicle, hanging my clothes on a peg, dipping a tin can in a bucket, and splashing the water over me as best I could. It had to be done quickly, for in that small space, and in that heat, the shower bath could quickly turn into a steam bath.

Later in the afternoon, our boat entered a long straight stretch of water where we could see for quite a distance ahead. In the bow was a tiny triangular platform. There Lyle, Edith, and I took up our lookout post. The pilot, who stood directly opposite us, called out his encouragement from time to time. Finally he raised his arm and pointed. "You can't see it yet—but about three miles more and we'll be in Cafetal."

We strained our eyes. We wondered what Jim might be wearing. We decided it would be either a white T-shirt or a bright-colored sport shirt, and khaki pants.

Slowly, the miles wore away. A palm roof over a red mud house came into view. Another and another . . . Then a knot of people standing on a high bank. We were too far away to pick out Jim's bald head from the others. Nor could we spot a tall figure, or T-shirt, or sports shirt. My heart sank. A lump came into my throat. Edith looked as if she were going to cry.

More houses came into view; then more people. The bell rang; the motor slowed; the boat shifted course toward shore. The group of people were closer now. Suddenly I saw a figure standing a head taller than the rest, then the unmistakable white T-shirt. I let out a shout: "There he is, honey! That's Jim, all right! And that's Helen standing right there next to him!"

Edith was jumping up and down, waving frantically. Tears came to our eyes. Jim and Helen must have seen us at about the same time, for they started waving excitedly, too.

As the boat pulled in they came running down the riverbank to meet us. Oh, what a melee of hugs and kisses and backslappings! We were so carried away by the emotion of our reunion that we were scarcely aware of the kindly, patient Bolivians who went about unloading our cargo and carrying it up the steep bank for us, and on to Jim and Helen's house.

Now that we knew Jim was safe, we could hardly wait to hear the whole story that had given rise to the rumors of his death. But this was not to be for awhile. The townspeople of Cafetal, curious to see the newcomers, swarmed through the house.

We learned quickly enough that it would be some time before we could have a home of our own. We would have to stay with Jim and Helen until we could build one.

Our gear was just about sorted out when we heard the boat's bell clang three times for full speed ahead. We went out to look; already the boat was far out on the broad expanse of the river. Soon it was a tiny speck fading into the distance.

"How soon will it be back?" I asked.

"Two weeks!" answered one of our new Bolivian neighbors.

A new, depressed feeling of loneliness and isolation came over us. For the first time we were discovering what most pioneer missionaries must experience at one moment or another, that sensation of being totally cut off. We were now truly on the edge of nowhere, dependent on our own resources, far from the comforts and diversions of civilization, out of touch with our loved ones at home. We could only pray to the Lord to bring peace to our hearts.

Helen's cheerful voice interrupted our gloomy reflections. "I'll have supper ready soon," she said.

How we were looking forward to it, our first change from a daily diet of rice and beans!

"I'm afraid it's going to be rather skimpy," she said apologetically. "Only beans and applesauce. Today we got right down to the bottom of our larder."

Beans again! But Helen managed to flavor them so they tasted different, at least, from the beans on the boat. We ate them all and my mouth was watering for the applesauce. Now Helen was even more apologetic. "I hope you can eat it," she said. "Knowing you might be coming, I spent the whole afternoon trying to pick the worms out of apples. But they were too much for me. In the end I had to give up and cook them—worms and all. I hope you don't mind too much."

When the dish was set before me I saw the worms, all right. My stomach underwent a minor revolt. I looked around out of the corner of my eye to see what Jim and Helen were doing. They were eating the applesauce with gusto. "If they can do it, I can too," I said to myself. By taking up a spoonful and not looking at it, at the same time trying hard to think of something else, I managed to get it down. So did Edith.

I was sustained by the thought of the provisions we had brought with us. This would be the last such meal we would have to face for some time to come.

We finished supper. Jim went over to the fire, picked out a smoking log, and put it under the table by our feet. I wondered whether he had gone off his rocker. Then I understood this was only good common sense: the smoke drove away the clouds of mosquitoes which were beginning to feast on our ankles and legs. This was our introduction to one species of the many insects that were to be our permanent house guests at Cafetal. Indeed, later experiences were to force me to conclude that it is not the dramatic dangers, the snakes, the quick mud, the deceitful savages, that try the soul of the pioneer missionary, so much as the ever-present pests—the mosquitoes, the ants, the reptiles, and the stinging, biting gnats.

Jim leaned back, making himself as comfortable as he could in a homemade chair. What most impressed me about him was his calm. With quiet detachment he recounted events to make one's hair stand on end, punctuating the narratives with bits of dry humor. Prematurely bald, probably as the result of some hard experiences in the military service—experiences of which he never spoke—he looked ten years older than his twenty-eight or so years.

The Bolivian visitors had stopped coming. We were alone and quiet. While the flickering light of the kerosene lamp cast our lengthened shadows on the wall, Jim began to talk. At last we were to hear his story—all that had happened in the blank spaces during the two years since we had last met in the States.

"I might as well begin at the beginning," he said, "so I'll start with the day I took off from Robore in the little Stinson plane. Mel Wyma was at the controls. It took us several hours to get here, but we had a good flight. The airstrip at Cafetal was new; Mel buzzed over it two or three times and it looked good, so we weren't worried. While Mel was here I enjoyed myself. But after a few days, he had to go on, leaving me all alone. Believe me, I never felt so lonely in my life. I only knew a few words of Spanish, so I couldn't make out what people were trying to say to me and I couldn't make myself understood. My imagination ran wild. I was sure the neighbors were plotting to do me in. Oh, how I wanted Helen to come and help me."

"Remember," Helen put in, "I spent some time in Mexico before I came to Bolivia, so I know Spanish pretty well."

"Besides that," Jim continued, "I needed someone to talk to. I tell you I was in despair. Once in awhile our Austrian friend, Frederico, would come in from the jungles. He speaks English, so he was a comfort; also, I got a lot of information. I don't know how accurate it is.

"One day, the twice-a-month mail boat stopped to drop off supplies. It was on its way to Matto Grosso, upriver in Brazil." He paused thoughtfully. "Here at Cafetal, you know, civilization—

if you want to call it that—comes to an end. Next stop—Matto Grosso—which picks up the thread again and carries it on into eastern and southern Brazil. There are a few settlements of rubber workers for a couple of days beyond here. Then for three days after that you go right through the heart of wild, unexplored territory—what they call the 'Green Hell.' You've read about Colonel Fawcett, haven't you? The British explorer who vanished in 1925?" I nodded. "That's where he disappeared. It's an unsolved mystery. Nobody knows what became of him. The stories around here are that he was killed by Indians."

I swallowed hard. "And these are the tribes we hope to reach with the Gospel?"

Jim nodded.

"Some of 'em. These are the Nhambiguaras. Hardly anything is known about them, except that they live today just as they did in the stone age. They even have axes made of stone. Some rubber worker gets a glimpse of them now and then running around naked. Or he doesn't see 'em at all and his body is found stuck full of arrows. But they never get close enough to talk to the Indians. So about all we have to go on is rumor . . . But to get back to my story:

"Frederico was off in the bush, panning gold by the Sansimoniano mountains. I'd reached the point where I could hardly stand it any longer. I'd almost made up my mind that when the boat came back from Matto Grosso I'd take it back downriver to Guajara Mirim and either come back with Helen, you, and Edith, or not come back at all.

"But when the boat did return, it brought with it a piece of news that put all thoughts of leaving out of my mind. To go then would have looked as though I were running away. Also, Frederico had come back, which eased my mind a bit.

"So here is the story, as Frederico translated it for me. As this mail boat, about three days after leaving Cafetal, was passing through the area known to be inhabited by the Nhambiguaras, it encountered a barricade reaching almost across the river. From the way it was made—with upright poles pounded into the river bottom and bound tightly together with ropelike bark—they knew it was the handiwork of Indians. The passengers were in a near-panic. They thought they were being ambushed. A narrow passage remained at one side with the water about chest deep, so the boat was barely able to snake through. As the boat passed, the crewmen lassoed the barricade and pulled a section of it loose."

We were sitting forward, listening intently. Just then the lamp gave a pop and a sputter, hissed and almost went out. We jumped. Helen and Edith squealed. Then we saw it was only a big moth that had fallen into the chimney. We laughed and let Jim go on with his story .

"But a few days later, when the mail boat passed that very spot on the return trip, they found that not only had the barricade been entirely rebuilt, but sharp spears were sticking out from it at deck level. If they had come on it during the night it could have been dangerous. Again the passengers were badly frightened.

"About ten miles farther downriver, they came on a Bolivian boy in a dugout, paddling with one arm. He appeared to have been wounded. When the mail boat drew closer they saw a body on the bottom of the dugout—a man dead, with four or five arrows in him. The crewmen took the boy aboard. He had an arrow still in his side. Fortunately, it wasn't poisoned. While they removed the arrow and dressed his wound, he told what had happened.

"He had gone with an older rubber hunter to find turtle eggs. They were getting ready to shove off when some natives appeared from the underbrush. The boy was seated in the bow. The older man jumped in to shove off, meanwhile shouting to the boy to leap into the water. The boy did so and that's probably what saved his life. He heard a couple of shots. The older man, remembering only then that he had a pistol, had fired at the Indians to frighten them away. But it was too late. He was already full of arrows. The boy helped the older man into the dugout and pushed out into the river. The man died within a few minutes.

"One arrow had struck the boy. He paddled with one arm and

drifted until we picked him up. The boat stopped at Rio Cabixi, a small settlement of rubber workers. There the man was buried and the boy was left to recover from his wounds."

Jim fell silent. Threads of smoke from the log curled up over the table. Just behind us, swarms of thwarted mosquitoes snarled an angry chorus.

"I suppose," Jim said, "that was how the rumor got started that I was the one who had been killed. Perhaps, too, it was because it happened not far from the spot where three missionaries had been killed in 1925. But how the rumor reached Guajara Mirim we'll never know."

Now Helen took up the story.

"That river trip up here was one I won't forget in a hurry," she said. "I was the only woman on the boat. The men were all very kind to me. But I felt so alone. It took us thirteen days—thirteen days of waiting and wondering, not knowing whether I would ever see Jim again. I just wouldn't let myself think about it. I put my trust in the Lord.

"But oh, that moment when I saw him standing there looking for me made up for everything. I threw my arms around him and kissed him and kissed him. I didn't care what the Bolivians thought. My emotions couldn't wait to ask questions."

Just then, from only a few feet away, came an enormous roar. We nearly jumped out of our skins. When we collected our wits, we saw it was only an old cow who had put her head in the window and sneezed.

"You'll get used to little surprises like that around here," said Jim, chuckling.

Our curiosity satisfied, weariness overcame us. We said goodnight and went to enjoy a night's sleep in a real bed for the first time in more than a week.

The next morning we had our first good look at the village which was to be our home. It was no more than a hole in the jungle. Thirteen or so palm-roofed houses straggled for a mile along the riverbank. The red earth of the paths and yards were in striking contrast to the solid green backdrop. The tangled vines made a living wall on every side, as though waiting patiently to take over. Before long our clothes took on a red tinge which we found hard to wash out.

Edith began visiting around with Helen and making friends with our Bolivian neighbors. It was a community consisting largely of women and children. The men were usually off in the jungle, tapping trees for the wild rubber. Every two or three months—usually before feast days—they would come roaring home. Pandemonium would break loose. The whole village was given over to dancing and wild drinking. Sometimes the celebrations would end in shootings. (Once, about a year after our arrival, a victim of one of these incidents ran for protection behind our house. Looking out the window, we saw bullets kicking up dust right in front of us.) There is no rule by government or police force in the small jungle settlements. The only law is "the fist, the whip, or the gun."

The slow beating of drums in the distance, accompanied by the shrill note of the fife, usually announced the beginning of the fiestas. Then we missionaries would stay close to our houses until it was all over.

The story of these families is a sad one. Most of the men had come out years before, from farms or towns in more civilized parts of the country, lured by dreams and rumors of sudden and fabulous wealth awaiting the adventurous in the "Green Hell" of the jungle. There were tales of hidden hoards of Inca gold, of diamonds as big as the end of your finger, of rare minerals and precious stones. On a more modest scale, they hoped to make money by finding *pualha,* a wild plant whose roots have mild narcotic properties and bring high prices.

As these dreams eluded them, they had to live. The only way they could make a steady living was to become rubber hunters. A few rich *patrones* controlled the trade. Everyone else worked for them at a few pennies a day, in a life of virtual slavery. Some *patrones* lived in Cafetal, too. But the world's goods were so scarce it was almost impossible to see any difference between the homes of the rich and those of the poor. All except one, which belonged to a *patrone*, had bare dirt floors, red earthen walls, and the meager essentials for furnishings. But most people were kind, courteous, and helpful.

A "well-to-do" home might have three or four straight-back red chairs, a hammock, a small table, and a sewing machine in the living room. One man had a kerosene refrigerator; two or three others had outboard motors. Because of these possessions they were considered wealthy.

The women did their cooking on the dirt floor over open fires. Two kettles and a frying pan comprised their kitchenware. For them, the height of prosperity was to be able to buy a pair of shoes from the privately owned commercial boat that stopped about every two months or so. They saved their shoes for Sunday. The rest of the time they wore sandals or went barefoot. All their worldly possessions could be kept in a foot locker. But everyone took pride in cleanliness. Whenever they went out, they wore their "Sunday best."

Our children's toys became the talk of the town. The women would gather around and exclaim over Connie's doll with the rubber skin and which could open and shut its eyes. Brian's mechanical duck, which could quack and raise and lower its wings to hit a little drum, was a subject of wonder. Grownups asked to pull it around on the dirt floor.

There was sorrow in many households over the frequent illnesses and death of children. It hurt our hearts because so many could have been saved with simple medicines or scientific care. There was none to be had.

The romance and adventure that marked our first days of missionary life were drawing to a close. Traveling, seeing new sights, hearing new sounds every day—all this was over. The work which had brought us here—reaching the savage tribes—still lay in the future. Our immediate concern was to settle in and get used to daily discomforts and privations, and to adapt as best we could to a new kind of life in an alien land.

5

Spearhead

In a couple of months we thought we should build our own mud house; we could not impose on Helen and Jim's hospitality forever. Having no money, I couldn't hire anybody to help me. But fortunately it was a much simpler matter than building a house in the States. You just put up crotched poles about nine feet tall to hold the cross pieces that will support the roof. For the wall, you fill in with other vertical poles, planted every two feet apart, then lash them together with horizontal strips of bamboo. This is the skeleton. Next you fill in with mud, which dries nearly as hard as cement—leaving space, of course, for windows and doors. Then you bring in hundreds and hundreds of palm leaves from the jungle, tie them on the long poles that reach from the walls to the peak of the roof like ribs, and a roof is made. For the floor you just slither around in a lot of wet mud, stomp it and smooth it out, and then let it dry. It has one advantage—no housewife ever worries about a visitor tracking in dirt.

I had a few tools, mainly an ax, a saw, and a machete. With these I made a wheelbarrow, cutting a more or less circular wheel out of a solid piece of wood, and went to work. I often smiled to myself as I thought that we must be living very much as our pioneer forefathers did. I built Edith a good workable wood stove by making my own bricks out of mud, baking them in the sun, then putting them together with more mud as mortar.

Three months after it was begun, the house was finally finished, and a happy day it was when we could begin our family life together under our roof.

Edith cooked many a delicious meal on the wood stove. For awhile we ate well from our stores; but we used these up with dismaying rapidity. We thought we could get our order filled in Cochabamba in about two months; but three months went by and our new provisions still hadn't come. We were down to almost nothing. There was no store where we could buy anything. For a couple of weeks it was nip and tuck. But neighbors brought us yucca, bananas, or fresh corn, and we got along.

One thing we had not anticipated was the array of insects and reptile life that enthusiastically moved in with us. We grew more or less accustomed to the ever-present mosquitoes. We learned to shake out our shoes and socks in the morning to dislodge the red scorpions that might be hiding there, capable of giving a nasty sting. But Edith never did get used to the cockroaches. She always let out an expression of disgust when she accidentally stepped on one, which was often. Perhaps this was a holdover from life in the Midwest, where the presence of cockroaches is considered a mark of bad housekeeping. In the tropics one has to learn to accept them as inevitable guests.

We got used to being on the lookout for poisonous snakes. The area had a number of deadly species: the little bright-banded coral snake, a small green snake (the name of which I never knew), and the nondescript but deadly tan-and-darker-brown Yoperrohobobo.

Especially did we watch out for the Yoperrohobobo after Helen told us what had once happened to her. She was lying on her bed taking a siesta when she saw a Bolivian peering in at her through the window. She thought this rude of him and was about to jump to her feet to tell him to go away. Instead he yelled at her to stay where she was, and not to move. He came quickly into the house with a machete in his hand, made a couple of swipes under the bed, and killed the Yoperrohobobo coiled there ready to strike.

One afternoon Connie was playing in the yard right outside our house. I heard her cry, "Ooh! Mommy! Daddy! Come see what I got!"

I went to the door of the house. She was jumping and laughing as she held a snake, about a foot-and-half long, by the tail. I was close enough to recognize the markings of the Yoperrohobobo. My heart sank into my shoes. Edith, beside me at the door, was absolutely frozen with horror, unable to move or utter a sound.

"Drop it! Drop it!" I shouted, and crossed the yard in one bound.

When I reached her I saw that the snake had a frog halfway down its throat—the only reason it had been unable to bite. We gave fervent thanks. It was only the Lord's protection that had saved her. We gave Connie a stern warning against picking up strange snakes and bugs.

Several weeks later we were having coffee one evening in our living room with a neighbor, a Bolivian woman, when she set down her cup and gave an exclamation of surprise in Spanish. Following her gaze, my eyes went to the top of the opposite wall where there was a space of about three inches below the pole rafters.

Pouring through and down the side like a living waterfall was a solid black curtain of army ants.

"*Gasolina! Gasolina!*" the woman cried. "It's the only thing that will stop them." She jumped up, then stopped. "No—wait—you can't do that. You might set fire to the house. Hurry. Wake the children. You've got to get out of here."

We snatched the sleepy children from their beds and scurried the hundred yards to the Ostewigs' house. We had to stop every now and then to stomp our feet to get rid of the stray ants, either real or imagined, that we felt crawling up our legs.

Early the next morning we returned to our home, wondering what we would find. There was not a movement, not a sound. Our food, which we kept in tight tin containers, and our clothing had not been touched. But the ants had killed, and taken with them the corpses of every living thing—bats, mice, spiders, cockroaches, and scorpions. Some of our neighbors who came around assured us that we need not expect another visit from the ants for another year or so.

For awhile we led a peaceful life absolutely free of pests—until in time they all moved back in again. I developed a friendly feeling toward those ants. They had done a job of house cleaning we could not have done ourselves. I was to have quite a different feeling, however, when I encountered them later on.

Weeks went by. Jim and I were growing impatient. We had not forgotten that we were here for a purpose—to bring the Word to primitive people who had never heard of Jesus Christ. We reviewed the long steps ahead: first, we would have to find out where the tribes were; next we would have to gain their friendship and confidence (which meant reversing a long history of warfare with the white man); then we would have to learn their language; and finally we could hope to teach them the Gospel and ways of Christian living. It was an undertaking that would require months, even years—indeed, one that we might never see bear fruit ourselves but might have to leave to those who came after us. But we were not disheartened at the prospect. We knew this to be the ordinary burden of the pioneer missionary.

What *did* bother us was that it was taking us so long to get started. There were no veteran missionaries in the neighborhood to whom we could turn for advice. We had no written reports, no maps, nor even any verbal information about the tribes we wanted to reach. This was truly the frontier, the front lines of all the powers fighting against us, physical as well as spiritual.

So we sought information in the only way we could. When the rubber workers came in from the bush, they often dropped over for a long evening of Bolivian coffee (and Edith's cookies). After their months of solitude it was not hard to get them to talk. Then we would put our heads together to try to sort out fact from fantasy and wild imaginings. There was enough of the latter to dampen any missionary's zeal: the tribes lived in a state of undeclared war with the nationals. The men said there was no doubt they were cannibals.

Our social evenings were time-consuming. Hours of conversational chaff might yield but one grain of dependable information. Put together, we had much that was useful. We learned, for example, that we had to calculate our timetable not by days, nor by weeks, but by seasons. Certain tribes could be reached best only in the dry season (April through November); others, when the river was at its flood. (And the lore we picked up from these seasoned veterans of the jungle literally saved our lives more than once.)

Typical of our informants was a gnarled *patrone* named Don Juan Camacho, who came on his first day back from upriver to spend the evening with us. Don Juan seemed to dread the razor blade. With most of his teeth gone and his lips sunk in, he looked as if he had missed catching a popfly. He wore an old pair of glasses which we thought he put on to make him look more dignified. He carried his sixty-some years of age with dignity as he strutted down the path with his full-blown trousers tucked into the top of his tattered boots. He had other men working for him in a little outpost on the edge of nowhere. Since he had survived economically, we knew he was both tough and knowledgeable.

I tried to explain to him the purpose of our mission. His black eyes looked at me with disbelief; a smile of sympathetic amusement played about his lips. The missionary viewpoint was so remote from his own he could hardly grasp it. From his shirt pocket he pulled out a cigarette paper, then reached in a small rubberized cloth pouch for his pungent, moldy-smelling tobacco. As he rolled his cigarette, he couldn't resist the remark, "You evangelicals don't smoke, do you? I don't think it's right, either, but have to do it to keep the mosquitoes away. *Asi es* [that's the way it is]." I looked for some mosquitoes and saw none. Jim and I smiled as he went on speaking.

"You'd have no trouble finding wild Indians," he said. "Not

far from here, about three days up the Guaporé near a place called Paredon—the red cliff—are the Nhambiguaras. They put that barricade in the river, you know."

My eyes must have brightened, for he said at once, "But I think you are crazy to try. Give it up, no? You're better off staying here trying to convert us. I don't want to be pulling your body out of the river someday."

Don Juan must have seen that his words were not making the desired impression, for his voice rose and he leaned forward in his straight chair: "You think perhaps because these Nhambiguaras are aborigines, you will be dealing with children, no? Well, I will tell you—they are clever—far more clever than we are. They are like shadows—like mist. They are never seen unless they want to be seen. But here—I will tell you a story—a true story of a short time ago, which will show you.

"A bunch of rubber workers—fellows that I know, I think there were eleven of them—go out hunting for turtle eggs. This is in Nhambiguara territory, so to be doubly safe, each one has a dog— eleven dogs. Also, they all have guns. You don't go into the jungle without your gun. Eleven men, eleven dogs, eleven guns. On the first night they make camp, not far from the river. They all climb into their hammocks. They all put their guns on the ground below them—within reach. The dogs sleep nearby. All peaceful, all quiet.

"In the morning they awake, feeling pretty good after a sound night's sleep. They rub their eyes and look around. Nothing. Stripped clean—food, pots, axes, machetes—everything gone. Even the guns are taken from under their hammocks. And not one dog barks.

" 'Sera?' ['Could it be so?'], I asked. (Later on the story was confirmed by others.)

"At that moment they hear the sound of mocking laughter. There, across the river on the sandbar, they see some Nhambiguaras waving the rubber hunters' guns; they are all doubled up, laughing themselves sick."

The patrone paused to relight his cigarette, which had gone out.

"*Asi es,*" he nodded. "It happens just like that. It is true. Maybe that gives you some idea of the people you will be dealing with. Not children, no? They are slick. Slick as shadows."

His weather-beaten face was solemn.

"One thing I must tell you while it is in my mind—if you persist in your foolishness, that is. If ever you are drawing near one of their camps or their villages and you come across an arrow in the trail—then don't go on. Do not stop to find out what it means. Just clear out—as fast as you can. You see, they are gentlemen in their way. That is their warning. They are telling you that you are not welcome—that if you do not leave at once, they will kill you." I was to remember that warning all too clearly.

We went on to ask him about other tribes. Well, yes, there were the Sansimonianos, another primitive tribe, living across the lowlands, beyond the mountains, some fifty miles to the west.

"About fourteen years ago," said the *patrone,* "there is a war— a real pitched battle—guns and bullets against bows and arrows. The Indians attack a small outpost of rubber hunters. The rubber hunters win. They kill a number of savages. Seven are captured and brought back here as servants."

I pricked up my ears.

"Since that time—nothing," the *patrone* went on. "Though they are so close, nothing is known of them. Only arrows now and then, coming out of the thickets, when some rubber worker goes too far into the wild country. *Asi es.*"

I had a chance to ask my question. "And what about the seven who were brought here?"

"Dead—all dead long ago. White man's diseases." He drew on his cigarette and thought a minute. "Wait a minute. No. There is one still living among us—although he keeps pretty much to himself."

"You mean right here in Cafetal?"

"Yes. Here in Cafetal. So why do I tell you about the Sansimonianos when you can get it all straight from his lips?"

Disgustedly, he tossed down his cigarette, which was always

going out. He stood up to say good-night. Our heads were reeling. How much of what he had told us was true? (Such as the tale of two hunters who had sat down on a log to rest, felt the log move, and found they were sitting on an enormous anaconda.) How much was an exaggeration or outright lie? At any rate, for the first time we had a clue—for action.

Next morning Jim and I set out to visit the Sansimoniano. We found him without much trouble. He lived all by himself in a miserable hovel at the edge of the village by the river. A wizened, stooped old man, his deep-lined face wore an expression of infinite sadness. He greeted us in fairly good Spanish, for he had learned the language by now. At first, he seemed friendly and well-disposed.

We squatted down on the ground and spoke to him slowly and patiently, trying to build up our case. We said we were missionaries and explained what a missionary was. We said we wanted to make friends with his people and to bring them the story of everlasting life. All this time his expression remained inscrutable. We could not tell how much he was comprehending. Then we said we would like to study with him for awhile, to learn some words and phrases of Sansimoniano, to learn something of the habits and customs of the tribe.

The Indian stood up. His dark eyes flashed defiance. "Never!" he exclaimed, and began to speak decisively. "Through the years many men have come and asked me this. The white man means only wickedness to my people. He wants only to kill them, enslave them, or do harm to them. That has been our history. No, I will never betray them. You will learn nothing from me. What I know will die with me."

We could only respect his feelings, although we knew that our first promising trail had come to a quick dead end.

It was the season of the year, more than anything else—and our growing impatience—that decided us to make a stab in the dark in an effort to reach the Sansimonianos.

The rains were diminishing, for we were now in April, the beginning of the dry season. Upriver, we were told, the Nhambiguara country along the river would still be under water. In a few more weeks the lowlands between us and the Sansimonianos would be so dry we would be in constant danger of running out of water. Without question, now was the season to go.

I have had many similar experiences since; but no period remains so emotionally vivid to me as those last few days before we set out on the trail for the first time. We were green hands and we knew it. All our ideas up to then about how we would survive in the jungle were entirely theoretical. Though we had rehearsed every conceivable situation over and over again—what we would eat, what we would wear, what to do in case of accident, what our first moves would be when we met the Indians—now came the first real test.

It was going to be hard on Helen and Edith. Daily life in Cafetal was tough enough with two able-bodied men to do the heavy work. But with their loved ones gone, facing the unknown, every day would be a trial, a renewed test of faith.

About this point our forces were strengthened by the arrival of a vigorous, energetic young missionary, a veteran bomber navigator named Ken Finney.

I smile each time I remember all the gear we took along on that first hiking trip: a hammock each, blankets, a change of clothing, sneakers for the swamp and work shoes for the high ground, provisions, utensils, and gifts for the Indians. Distributed among the three of us, each pack weighed about sixty pounds—quite a load for that rough country. We had several pounds of rice tied in a bag, oatmeal, salt, powdered milk, and a little Nescafé. Our most valuable item was one we had picked up from the Bolivians, a kind of cereal that could be eaten either dry or with water or milk. We made this ourselves by parching corn, grinding it quite coarse, and mixing it with equal parts of ground peanuts and a little salt. This proved to be very handy to have when it was too wet to build a fire. The rice was something else again. It was bland and tasteless. Hungry though we were, there were times when we could hardly stomach it. It took us many trips before we learned that flavorings of various kinds, for example, bacon fat, or spices such as poultry seasoning, were as necessary as the rice itself.

Our farewell was a difficult one made all the harder by the fact that Brian didn't understand why we couldn't take him, too. Long after we were alone in the jungle stillness, the beloved voices calling "Bye-bye, Daddy" and "Good-by, sweetheart" rang in my ears.

At first we walked along a path wide enough for an oxcart, between two high solid walls of jungle growth. Embracing overhead, these walls made us feel we were going through a tunnel. The damp air was at least ten degrees cooler than at Cafetal. But the water had not gone down as much as we counted on. Soon we were waist-deep in it, stepping over logs and hoping none of them would turn out to be an anaconda. Once Jim and I, who were in the lead, noticed that Ken was suddenly silent. We turned and saw only his hat floating on the water. But before we could become alarmed, he popped up, choking and sputtering.

Just when we were beginning to wonder how much more of this we could take, we came out into the *campo* (grassland). A few more hours, and we saw before us a little clearing and a farm, a lonely outpost in the middle of nowhere. The farmer, a smiling, toothless Bolivian rubber worker, came out to greet us. How glad we were to see him and how glad the family were to see us! They invited us to stay the night. When we left in the morning, they pressed on us half the food they had—fresh eggs, pineapples, and so on, real delicacies to us. The Bolivian insisted that he go along with us as a guide, taking his ox with him. We were happy to accept, for the straps of our heavy packs were cutting into our shoulders. Now we could put the packs on the animal's back for awhile. As we went, the Bolivian showed us a scar on his shoulder. A few years before, he had ventured too far from his farm and was shot with an arrow.

At the end of the third day, the *campo* came to an end. From here we faced more swamps and more and more rivers to cross.

Our guide informed us regretfully he could go no farther. Wishing us well, he turned home again with his ox. We were again on our own.

The mountains beyond the swamps seemed so near and yet came no nearer. The ground grew wetter and wetter; we were becoming exhausted from the heat and the weight of our packs. Once, when Jim thought he saw signs of an old Indian trail, we took heart. But it turned out to be a false clue.

Every fourth day we decreed a day of rest. We spent more time than normally reading the Bible and also in regaining our strength. On one of these rest days, Jim went to put on his shoes. He banged them together, as we had learned to do almost automatically in case a snake or a scorpion were within. Nothing came out, so he slipped his foot inside. He let out a terrific howl. He had been stung by a scorpion right through his sock. In training, we had been taught to identify types of scorpions: this one, fortunately, was not the deadly variety. But Jim was in an agony of pain for twenty-four hours. Out there in the jungle there was nothing we could do for him, except to try to divert his mind from it with reading and talking.

With so much flooded jungle ahead of us, we changed direction and headed south toward some nearer mountain peaks. This turned out to be the right course, for we were soon in dry grasslands at the very foot of the mountains.

We found a good place to make camp. We had to decide whether to push on or go back. We had been gone nearly three weeks and our staple supplies were getting low. Contrary to our expectations, we had been unable to shoot any game. We had not so much as seen one wild animal or one wild bird. But we did not like to return defeated. We finally agreed to make one last try to find a trace of the Sansimonianos. Two of us would climb the mountain; one would stay in camp. We drew straws and Jim remained. Ken and I started our climb.

We made our way around the slope where I could see to draw some maps of other mountain ranges. I was sketching them when Ken grabbed me by the arm.

"Look!" he cried. "Right down below us! In that small valley! I see the smoke from some campfires!"

"No doubt about it," I replied. "Must be a hunting party of Sansimonianos."

It was already late in the afternoon; the sun was sinking low behind the distant mountains. Darkness would have fallen by the time we reached the encampment of the Indians. Did we dare come up on them at that hour? On the other hand, we might not have such an opportunity again soon. If we waited until morning, the Indians might be gone. We decided it would be foolhardy to try to reach them now—better wait for daylight.

Ken and I headed back down the mountain to rejoin Jim. Twilight gave way to darkness. Groping our way over the *campo* in the pitch black was quite a different experience from finding our way in the daytime. The arrangement was that Jim would keep shining his flashlight to guide us. Often we mistook the fireflies for the gleam of Jim's light in the distance! But at last there it was—waving up and down.

When we returned, Jim had supper ready. As we ate, we told him the events of the day. We were exhausted, so fell into our hammocks early.

At the first streak of dawn, with our packs left behind, we hiked off toward the valley. In an hour or so we came upon the encampment. We found the Indians had covered up all evidence of their presence, even their fires. Scattering, we eagerly searched the jungle wall for signs of a trail. But this tribe left no telltale mark behind them.

Once more we took stock of our situation. Barely enough food remained to see us back to Cafetal. There was no choice now: we would have to give up on this trip. Again disappointment—and a bitter one, when we had come so close. But at least we knew the Sansimonianos were here. Someday we would reach them.

Our lightened packs made the homeward journey easier. We quickened our steps as we recognized the clearing that was Cafetal. Looking at one another, we became aware of our shabby appearance for the first time and laughed. Bearded, gaunt, caked with mud up to our belts, we were a sorry crew.

But our welcome could not have been more heartfelt.

Helen and Edith had been visited daily by well-meaning Bolivian neighbors, who, wanting to be solicitous, only increased their concern with such statements as:

"Your men should be home by now."

"We fear they have run out of food."

"Perhaps the *tigres* have eaten them."

"They should not have tried to meet those savages."

To all of them, Helen and Edith had replied with unshaken faith, "They will come." But it had been hard on them.

Oh, how good it was to smell the aroma of cooking bacon and eggs, and the faint fragrance of cologne, assurance of the presence of loved ones! How good to know that we would have at least a few days at home before being called once more to the trail!

6

Catapulted into the Stone Age

On the whole we had a pleasant few months following our trip into Sansimoniano country. We had made friends with our Bolivian neighbors, and hardly a night went by that our house was not filled. We tried reaching them with the Gospel. Those who'd had any religion at all had left it far behind in their youth and were happy to hear stories from the Bible again. Above all, they loved singing with us in Spanish the lively evangelical hymns, such as "There Is Power in the Blood" and "Ye Must Be Born Again." Often we would sing the same song over and over again.

We learned of another way of reaching the Sansimonianos and decided to try it. This meant going some distance downriver, beyond a certain river junction. Following this route we could travel by water to the area we had hiked to before.

We left and were gone for an uneventful four weeks. Then the outboard motor broke down and our supplies began to run low. Again we had to return with nothing to show for our efforts.

One evening our friend Don Juan Camacho came to call. "If you are still bent on making contact with the Nhambiguaras," he said, deftly rolling the paper for one of his endless cigarettes, "now is the time to do it. *Asi es.*"

Edith asked him on what he based his reasoning.

"It is August now. The peak of the dry season approaches," said the *patrone,* with his sleepy smile. "This is the season of the year when the sandbars are highest and driest, and the turtles go there to lay their eggs. Mmm—they are good—no?

"So—that is also the time when the Nhambiguaras go to the riverbank to hunt the eggs. I would like to hunt some myself—if I had the time."

We laughed, knowing he had all the time in the world if he wanted to go.

"So that is your best chance to meet these wild men face to face—if you are still bent on committing suicide. Ah . . . those Nhambiguaras, they are wily ones," he sighed, blowing a long cloud of heavy blue smoke toward the roof.

He went on to tell more of his lurid tales—of suspected cannibalism, of the bodies of rubber workers found full of arrows, of rubber workers who had mysteriously vanished, leaving no trace.

We could hardly sleep that night. The next day Jim and I started at once to lay plans for an expedition. But one thing and another delayed our departure. Ken Finney had left us to attend to mission business in Cochabamba. In the meantime, we were pleased to learn that a young missionary couple named Bob and Betty Williams were coming to join us, and we waited for their arrival.

It was well into October before we were ready to start. Neither the *patrone's* stories nor the even wilder tales of other Bolivian neighbors deterred us. We were fully mindful of the risks. But to us the Nhambiguaras were souls in need of salvation.

Finally Jim Ostewig, Bob Williams, and I loaded the last of our provisions into the dugout. Waving good-by to our families, we chugged off upriver on our mission.

After waiting without success for Indians to appear at the sandbars, we decided to go inland. Perhaps we might find one of their villages. With no idea how far we might have to travel, we hid our outboard, gasoline, guns, and camera. Into our packs we stuffed enough food to last a little over a week.

It was a bright, hot morning when we set out to find their trail. Almost immediately this proved an exasperating business. The only promising signs were the twigs the Indians had bent on the trees to guide them on the way back inland to their villages. But it soon became clear they had no interest in traveling in a straight direction. We came on a faint trail. But it zigzagged and crisscrossed. Whenever the Indians had come to a tangle of jungle vines, they never hacked their way through, but crawled under it. We made many twists and turns, now losing one trail, then picking up another.

The silence around us was broken only by the twittering of birds and the crashing of our own bodies through the brush. After awhile we came out in an open place, a bare patch where the grass was burned off. In a way this was a relief: for the first time we could see some distance ahead, and we were no longer fearful of walking into an ambush.

But the Nhambiguaras had burned the section, we assumed deliberately, in order to destroy their bent-over twigs or trampled leaves and thus hide their whereabouts. We traveled by compass, hoping to pick up their trail later on beyond the *campo*. Unshaded, it was fiercely hot. We had found no water for hours and were sweating profusely in the broiling sun.

I noticed Bob was not saying much. His face was flushed and his eyes glassy. Finally he admitted he felt quite ill. He thought he had come down with a bad case of flu. But there was no water to be found here in the *campo;* we had to keep going.

By four o'clock both Jim and I were also exhausted. We could only imagine how much worse Bob, lightheaded with his fever, must feel.

Coming to jungle again, we found a small path leading down into a wooded glen. Since the tracks seemed to have been made by animals rather than by men, we hoped it might take us to a water hole. We quickened our pace.

Yes, there was the water hole, all right. But to our deep disappointment, it had dried up. There was only a circle of caked, dry mud.

Bob sank to the ground with a moan. "I'm sorry, fellows," he said. "I can't go on."

Jim and I grabbed our machetes. This might be our only chance to drink, and we had to make the most of it. With our waning strength, we began to dig feverishly. About two feet down, to our great delight, we found water. It was muddy and sour to the taste— and oh, what a stink! But it was water, and with no human life about, there was no chance of its being contaminated. We had to restrain ourselves from drinking more than was good for us. After the first few gulps we sipped; we filled up our kettles and canteens for drinking and cooking. I got the idea I'd like to have a bath! How refreshing it would be. Digging down a little deeper, I scraped up another two or three cupfuls and splashed them over me. This did more for my morale than any needle shower in a modern hotel.

Since Bob was unable to go on, we had to make camp where we were. We didn't want to build a fire, lest the smoke attract attention to our presence. But we had to eat to keep up our strength, so we made one. The rice tasted so sour from the water that Jim and I could hardly stomach it. Bob didn't touch his.

After an uneasy night, we were glad to see the dawn. The jungle was noisy with screaming parrots. Refreshed by the food and water and a night's rest, Jim and I felt glad to be alive. But Bob was still very sick. It was tantalizing to have come so far over the hard trail, perhaps even close to our goal, only to be unable to go on. We talked over the situation. None of us wanted to give up. Yet Jim and I felt we couldn't leave Bob alone; we had better all stick together. We bowed our heads and prayed for guidance. Then we put it up to Bob. He would have to decide. It was a hard choice for him to make. He was quiet for a long time. At last he spoke: "I think I feel a little stronger now. Let's go on as far as we can. When I can't make it any farther, we'll stop."

We picked up our packs and pushed on again. Before long we

came on a well-beaten trail beside a tiny stream. Perhaps the trail would lead us to a village. (We were beginning to understand something about the Indians. When they were near the main river, they deliberately made their trails hard to follow; farther inland, they felt safer and didn't seem to mind leaving them clearly marked.)

Our ears were kept alert for any strange sounds, while our eyes searched the path ahead for any possible arrows stuck there as warning. Since we were unarmed and deep in the Indians' own territory, we knew we were at their mercy. We proceeded in this way for about an hour. Bob grew weaker and stumbled more frequently. He could not go much farther.

I let out a smothered cry of joy. Ahead of us was a small clearing. We could see no huts or houses. But we did see plants growing under cultivation: yucca, broad-leaved young banana trees, and a small patch of corn. The sight left no room for doubt—we had come on an Indian farm. But not a human being was to be seen anywhere.

Bob stretched out on the ground. "You fellows go on," he said. "I'll stay here and rest."

We strung his hammock between two trees and made him as comfortable as we could.

"We'll scout around for a couple of hours, then we'll come back for you," I said as we left.

Proceeding very slowly, Jim and I walked out into the open space and crossed the newly planted farm. On the other side of the clearing we again picked up a well-beaten path. Following it for about half an hour, we came to another clearing with about eight crude, conical huts. We had found what we were looking for: a Nhambiguara village.

For a few minutes we waited in the deep shadows on the edge of the jungle. A deathly stillness lay over everything. After what seemed a lifetime, I was unable to bear the suspense any longer. I let out a lusty shout. At the far side of the clearing, an Indian appeared. Quite tall, with long black hair and fierce black eyes, he was altogether naked. In one hand he held a long bow and about a dozen arrows.

We stared at each other without moving.

What a moment that was! Before us stood the first living, aboriginal Indian we had ever seen. He must have looked exactly as his primitive ancestors did. I felt he and I were staring at each other across three thousand years!

Judging by his expression, which was a mixture of astonishment, curiosity, fear, and anger, I think we must have appeared as strange to him as he to us.

He spoke first, in a rapid series of guttural ejaculations totally incomprehensible to us. I longed for some way to tell him that we had come to bring friendship and love. But how to convey our feelings? I tried saying something—but it had no more meaning for him than what he was saying had for us. I felt frustrated, hopelessly separated from him.

The Indian began to wave his arm in a semicircular motion, indicating that he wanted us to follow him into the woods.

What did he mean by that gesture? "Come and join our party"? Or, "Let's get acquainted"? Maybe it was, "I want you to meet the others." Or quite possibly, "Come closer—so we can kill you more easily." That gesture could have any one of a hundred meanings. We stayed where we were. The Indian stepped back slowly and was swallowed by the jungle.

After a brief hesitation, Jim and I walked out into the clearing. When we reached the first hut, we knelt down and peered in the doorway, which was so low one could enter only on one's hands and knees. I started to crawl in.

"Better not," warned Jim. "They could trap us there."

Glancing inside, I saw only a bare earthen floor on which were three rocks presumably used for cracking palm nuts or building a fire, a basket or two, and a bow and arrow. What a bleak picture of elemental life! This must be a people, I thought, who are forced to live mostly on the trail in the unending search for food.

I heard a rustling in the leaves. Jim and I hurried across the clearing to a lean-to on the side from which we had just come. This gave us shelter from the sun. From here we could survey the scene, and make our escape quickly if we had to. We spent something like two hours here. The uneasy feeling that unseen eyes were boring into our backs prompted us to leave. We went back down the jungle path to rejoin Bob.

At the sight of us, he almost wept for joy. "I thought you'd never come back," he said. "Every minute I've been wondering what's happening to you—if you're still alive, and what I'd do if you were killed. I tell you—this experience convinced me of one thing: if we're going to die, let's all die together."

"We came to the same conclusion," Jim said with a nod.

Before we could tell what we had seen, Bob had an adventure of his own to recount. "You had just gone," he said. "I was lying here with those dark thoughts coming up in my mind when I heard a rustling. Close by—right near our packs. I looked up from my hammock and saw two naked Indians standing there staring at me. They lifted up their bows and drew them back. Wow, was I scared! They were pointing their arrows straight at me. Man, I thought for sure my hour had come. They stood there like that for a minute, and then you wouldn't believe what happened. Slowly, their arms relaxed; they didn't let their arrows fly. I'm sure the Lord stopped 'em from shooting."

He paused to get his breath.

"Then the two of 'em ran off and disappeared. I went to our packs and got some knives and rice. I left the stuff on the ground for a gift if they came back. I was pretty scared they would. Look at this note. It's a farewell note to my wife. I wrote it then. I figured in case anything happened to me, maybe somebody'd find it and get it out to her. But they never came around again. The stuff's still out there."

In our eagerness to reach the village we had forgotten, until now, that the Bolivians had told us the Indians are terribly vulnerable to such white man's diseases as the flu. We reproached ourselves. We should have thought of this before.

Reluctantly, we decided to call an end to this expedition and try to find our way back to the river. Bob felt he was barely strong enough to travel. We left the gifts behind and consoled ourselves by thinking they might pave the way for a later contact.

Jim walked in front, then Bob, then I. We had not gone far on the jungle trail when something pricked me in the leg. I stopped and leaned over to pick it up. It was the head of an arrow, made of bamboo, about a foot long and sharpened to a needle point. It was stuck in the path, pointing toward us. Don Juan's warning resounded in my ears. We hurried on.

A mile or so farther, we came on another sign of their hostility. A log was lying across the path. Stepping over it, I came down hard on what looked to be a pile of leaves. Beneath the leaves was a cluster of four-inch thorns. Fortunately, I had on heavy-soled work shoes! Nevertheless, one thorn did pierce the sole and enter my foot. It was a trap set for us by the Nhambiguaras. Since for the most part even the nationals go barefoot in the area, it was meant to be crippling. I waited to feel a sting around my wound. There was none, so I concluded that the thorns had not been poisoned. We kept going.

The open stretch of grasslands was a welcome sight. At least it indicated we were headed in the right direction. But after crossing the burned-over patch, we lost the last trace of any trail. In the wall of jungle on the other side, it was impossible to find our marked place of entry. We could rely only on our compass and plunge ahead.

Once more we were tormented by thirst. Our water from a creek by the Nhambiguara village had long since been exhausted. In our haste we had crossed the open, pitilessly exposed spaces of the campo at a much faster pace than usual. So although we were in the cool of the jungle, we were paying the penalty with our burning thirst.

Never have I known a worse sensation. My tongue swelled and seemed to fill my throat, giving me the panicky feeling that I was about to choke. Our strength ebbed. Every few minutes one or the other of us would fall and lie there on the ground, unable to go on. The craving, craving for moisture consumed me. I began to have hallucinations, seeing things that weren't there, such as a cooling waterfall. As one of us fell, the others encouraged him to get up and try again. When I dropped, I understood how simple it would be just to lie down and die right there.

With only our compass to point us in the general direction of the river, we plunged blindly through thorns and undergrowth. Our shirts and trousers were torn to shreds; our bodies were covered with scratches.

I felt I could go no farther. I was about to slide to the ground when I saw at my feet a long, cup-shaped palm leaf. Held in its curved service was a little pool of moisture. At first I thought it was only another mirage. Slowly, I grasped the fact that it was real.

Then came the test. The impulse just to gulp and gulp selfishly, before Jim and Bob could get any, was strong. But the bonds of brotherhood and love, forged and tempered by the hardships of the trail, were stronger. With great self-restraint, we each took a tiny sip in turn and then waited for the other. The water was full of wrigglers. But that didn't deter us in the least. There were about three cupfuls altogether. We swallowed its cooling refreshment, wrigglers and all. How good it felt on our parched throats and tongues! Then we all knelt down and gave thanks to the Lord for His mercy. The words of Isaiah 41:17, 18, came to our lips: "When the poor and needy seek water, and there is none, and their tongue faileth for thirst, I the Lord will hear them, I God of Israel will not forsake them."

How many simple blessings in life we take for granted because they are always there. Only when we are deprived of them can we give them our full appreciation. All my life I had given thanks for food. Ever since that experience I have given thanks for water also.

Refreshed and renewed, we resumed our struggle through the thorns. We had gone only a few steps when Jim let out a joyful shout: "Hey, fellows! We've found it."

We hurried to catch up with him. He was bending over a footprint in the earth—a clear footprint made by a shoe, pointing to the way in which we had come. We had found our own trail.

From then on it was fairly easy going, until we reached the riverbank and threw ourselves on the sand. We drank and drank, as though we would drink the Rio Guaporé dry.

There on the bank we sat to rest and review our experiences of the last few crowded hours. We felt we'd done enough for one trip. The warning of the pointed arrow had to be taken seriously. It would be crazy to go again soon into Nhambiguara territory. Besides, Bob was still weak from the flu.

After one sound night's sleep, we loaded our dugout with the few provisions that remained and headed downriver for Cafetal.

7

Digging In

December had ushered in the rainy season. For some distance
back from the banks, the jungles on either side of the river were under water. We knew we would have to wait six or seven months,
until the flooded areas had completely dried up, before making another effort to reach the Nhambiguaras. It was one of those periods
of just waiting and making plans that appear often in the life of a
pioneer missionary.

In January, 1951, the opportunity came to break the monotony:
a one-month trip to Cochabamba for the New Tribes Mission's
annual field conference, attended by most of our missionaries in
Bolivia. It proved a time of spiritual refreshment. Living as we
had been on that primitive outpost of civilization for almost a year,
there had been no opportunity to attend the Sunday or midweek
services to which we had been accustomed back home. I had not
realized how much I missed the fellowship of prayer and hymn
singing until our first service at the conference. When the hearty
voices first burst into song, I could not hold back the tears.

This was also a time for evaluation of our work. I had to report
to the conference that we did not have much to show for our efforts

so far. But our hearts were still full of hope for the future.

Not long after Edith and I and the Ostewigs were back home in Cafetal, we were cheered by the arrival of another missionary, Dave Yarwood, who had come out to help us in our work. Dave looked like a big, ambling bear. He gave the impression of being rough, tough, and ready for anything. But he had a heart as soft as butter. Dave was a bachelor. He had a widowed mother back in the States, to whom he wrote faithfully. Having grown up as a farm boy in Washington State, he was used to the out-of-doors and loved to hunt and fish. (In the months we were on the trail together, often in danger, with each other's welfare on our conscience, Dave and I were to become closer than most brothers.) Dave didn't relish sitting around idly in Cafetal. As we talked things over, it became clear that there was at least one thing we could accomplish during this floodtime: we could locate a piece of high ground on which to build a permanent forward base for further contact work with the Nhambiguaras. This would overcome the need to return to Cafetal every couple of weeks for supplies.

About the middle of February I loaded the dugout with gasoline for the outboard and with staple foods. Dave wanted to take with him his little black dog, a mongrel with shiny black hair which he had picked up in Guajara Mirim and brought along to Cafetal. He called the dog "Sacky" because it was always crawling into the sack with him. We also brought one other dog, thinking they would help guard us against surprise attack by the Indians. When the mail boat came, to save gas we hitched our canoe behind it. Jim and I said good-by to our families and took off upriver with Dave. Bob had returned to Cochabamba.

About the third day we thought we passed the spot where we had followed the trail inland to the Nhambiguara village. I say "thought" because the old sandbar was now deep under water and the place was hardly recognizable.

A few miles farther on we signaled the pilot to slow down so we could cast off. Then, the outboard purring, we were on our own, our eyes alert for the first piece of high ground. We had not gone far when we saw a reddish expanse of cliff rising about fifty feet on the Bolivian side. This was our landmark; we had reached Paredon. Jim leaned on the tiller and we headed for shore.

We made our first camp in the mud right by the riverbank. Exploring would be left for another day. Jim, Dave, and I were glad enough to get into our hammocks that night; at least we were off the muddy ground and protected against the frequent downpours by being zipped into our jungle hammocks, under our tarpaulins.

Everything was soggy. When the rains came, it was without warning and in a deluge. In the days that followed, as we set up our camp, we expended a good deal of energy trying to find dry wood to keep a fire going, then stoking it up hot enough to cook on. The ground all around us was a slithering, muddy mess.

Only at night in our hammocks would we be dry. But the army had no thought for comfort when the jungle hammock was designed. We slept in jacknife shape, our heads and feet above the rest of our bodies. We awoke feeling more stiff and weary than refreshed.

One morning when the rain let up we went hunting for a campsite. We thought we found an ideal location: the hill above the rust-red cliff from which Paredon took its name. On the high ground the packed dirt, unlike the silt farther down, would not turn into a sea of ooze when we tramped around on it. It was an impenetrable tangle of trees, vines, and thick foliage, but that didn't bother us. Several days of hard work with ax and machete would take care of that.

"Hey!" It was Jim's voice calling. "Come take a look." He was standing near the brow of the cliff, the black Rio Guaporé rolling by at his feet. The lowering clouds lightened for a moment, disclosing in the distance the faint blue line of the Brazilian uplands.

"Way over there. I think that's the Nhambiguara village where we saw the Indian that day."

"How about that!" I exclaimed. "You're right! And I doubt if it's more than a day's hike from here."

Heartened by our discovery, we slipped and slithered back down the hill and began sharpening our tools for the hard job ahead.

It was now late morning and we were pretty hungry. I was going through the usual routine, trying to find wood and tease it into burning so we could cook our noonday meal, when I heard Dave call, "Hey, Bruce! Look over there by the jungle!"

I straightened up. I saw something which had not been there a few moments before. At first I thought it was a shadow—long and wide—along the ground. But it could not be a shadow—for there was no sun. Then I saw it was moving, moving at a slow, steady pace, directly toward me. The whole ground seemed to be in motion, heaving, swaying. Almost automatically, my eye went to the edge nearest me. From there little black rivulets of the mysterious shape ran out, moving more rapidly than the main tide, but in no set direction; they zigzagged this way and that. Then I knew.

"Ants!" bellowed Dave, almost at the same moment.

"Army ants!" I echoed.

Into my mind flashed the memory of that awful evening in Cafetal when ants had come pouring down into our house like a waterfall. In my imagination I could see the mass invasion reaching back into the jungle—how far? "For miles, sometimes," the Bolivians had said.

The main column was no more than fifteen feet away.

"Come on Dave, Jim—let's get out of here!" I yelled. We ran for our dugout at the river's edge.

As we went, I began to get angry. We could escape with our skins. But this would mean the end of our forward base. Once the ants had discovered our sugar—not to mention our beans— they would settle in for good. Then we could kiss our camp good-by. And just when we had discovered our ideal location.

I remembered our neighbor's suggestion in Cafetal: the gasoline torch. I made up my mind we were not going to be routed by a bunch of ants.

"Come on, fellows!" I called. "We're going to give 'em a fight."

Grabbing a five-gallon can of gasoline from the dugout, I started back. "Quick! Find some cups or cans! Get some matches!"

The crisscrossing ribbons of ants were almost at the campsite. These were the reconnoitering troops, which sent back signals to the main army as to which way to advance. My skin crawled as I watched. Already, in my fancy, I could feel the nasty little feet all over my body, the myriad nips from their strong, hard pincers. Was it true, as I had heard, that enough of them could eat all the flesh off a man in minutes?

Jim was holding out a metal cup, Dave a tin can. With trembling hand, I filled them with gasoline. They threw the contents to the ground in front of the ants and tossed a lighted match after it.

There was a *pouf!* followed by an orange flash, and the muddy ground began to burn merrily. The advance guard wavered. But already the fire was flickering out. The main column moved on. More gasoline—more flames—again and again . . . We watched to see the results. I looked at Dave and Jim. Their faces, eerily ruddy in the reflection of the flames, were masks of fascinated awe. Finally we saw the main body pause, then march in perfect formation back into the jungle.

Abruptly, we sat down on the nearest packing cases to mop our brows. We were sweating—and not only from the heat. It was some time before our appetites returned. I resumed preparing the noonday meal.

About midafternoon, some sixth sense caused me to glance toward the north. "Not again!" I shouted. Sure enough, there came the same shadow. The ants were marching back from another direction—this time with a difference. No wavering ribbons came zigzagging ahead. They had dispensed with the reconnoitering troops and were coming much faster. It was not sugar they were after now; they were after us!

In the measured speed of their approach I could feel a determined malevolence, a brutal, silent, menacing, single-minded purpose.

But this time we were ready for them.

I had just touched off the first flash when Dave called out:

"Here comes another column from the other side!" Indeed, they were attacking on two fronts.

For the next few minutes we splashed gasoline and kept the fire blazing in wide semicircles. Wave after wave came up, climbing over the bodies of their incinerated comrades. They continued on relentlessly. Ruefully, we watched our fuel supply go down and down. But slowly the message seemed to reach the ants that they were up against a raging inferno. Again the columns reversed themselves and marched off into the jungle.

One direction, however, they had not yet tried: the south. We ate our supper uneasily, expecting the long shadow to reappear. At length, exhausted by our efforts, we fell into our hammocks. But we did not sleep much that night. Every now and then one of us would shine his flashlight through the mosquito net and along the ground to see if the silent, deadly column were approaching.

For the next few days, as we improved the camp, we were on edge. But the ants did not reappear. Apparently, our "scorched earth" policy had done the trick.

The weather, which had worsened, lifted a little again and so we were able to attack the undergrowth atop the cliff. But gasoline was low, and so was food. We rationed our beans and rice for awhile; but we grew so weak we could not do a good day's work. Finally, we reached the point where we had to go back to Cafetal to replenish our stores and rest up.

After two weeks at home, we returned to our task. We were stronger now, and had enough rations to last seventeen days. The rains had diminished, and we could go about the job of building our camp in earnest.

The hardest part was cutting the mahogany logs—they were from four to six inches in diameter—and hauling them in from the jungle with ropes made of braided vines. We dug and set these into the ground, making a kind of stockade which enclosed a fairly large room. Now, at least, we would have some protection from the arrows of a surprise attack. Above this we lifted a ridge pole the length of the "house," held in place by a vertical log with a crotch at each end of the house. From the center ridge pole we tied long two-inch saplings that came down at a forty-five-degree angle to rest atop the side walls. On these riblike saplings, two feet apart, we tied the soggy palm leaves.

When we stood back to survey our handiwork, we had to admit it wasn't much to look at. It would have hardly passed muster as a ramshackle barn back home. But it was an outpost.

We squatted on the cleared ground and held a council. From our vantage point we could see that much of the low-lying jungle country on the Brazilian side of the river was still flooded and would remain so for some time to come. There would be no point in even trying to make another contact until the latter part of August, five months away.

"Why don't we try another friendly contact with the Sansimoniano tribe?" I suggested. "If that is successful, we'll stay with it. If not, then we can come back here. In the meantime we'll get some more experience out on the trail." The others agreed.

We received plenty of experience indeed during the next three months of expedition deep into the jungles west of Cafetal. But the Sansimonianos eluded us.

Now we knew we must put all our efforts and heart into trying to reach the Nhambiguaras in a friendly way. We never dreamed of what we would face.

8

New Beachhead

One hot August afternoon, after we were back at Paredon, Jim, Tom, Dave, and I got into our dugout and went hunting for turtle eggs. About a month before, Tom Moreno, a young missionary from Texas, had come upriver to join us. Tom was about twenty; he had the marvelous stamina of youth and a winning way with everyone he met.

Turtle eggs, soft-shelled and about the size of ping-pong balls, are nearly all yolk. The nationals consider them a great delicacy. They either eat them raw or boil them to make a cooking oil. These methods did not appeal to us, because of the egg's rather grainy consistency. But we had found out they fluffed up well to make a very fine omelet, tasting much like chicken eggs with a slight fishy flavor. Also, they were very high in protein, an invaluable source of energy when one is working and exploring.

Over on the Brazilian side of the river lay a huge sandbar of perhaps five acres. Such sandbars usually are formed where the river takes a bend. This one looked like an ideal place for turtles to lay their eggs, so we beached the canoe and started our hunt.

We spread out in order to cover as much territory as possible in our search for the small, sharp prints of the turtles' claws, which might lead us to the spot where the eggs had been deposited under the sand.

Suddenly Dave let out a whistle. "Hey!" he called in a low voice. "This is no turtle print! Come here."

We ran to where he stood, his huge bulk bent almost double. He was peering intently at the sand. There, unmistakably, was a human footprint—and a fresh one at that.

"It was made by an Indian—I'm sure of it!" Jim whispered with awe.

Back in Cafetal, Don Juan had briefed us on how to tell the footprint of an Indian if we ever came across one: it would be characteristic of a person who had gone barefoot all his life—very wide at the ball of the foot, with the toe marks distinct and spread out. This one filled the bill exactly.

Turtles forgotten, we deployed and began our hunt anew. More prints turned up—then more and more.

As we followed different sets of tracks, we were surprised to find ourselves converging at the same point on the edge of the brush.

Peering into the thicket, we saw signs of a new-made trail. Although fully mindful of the dangers, we decided to make the most of our discovery.

The trail was fairly easy to follow. Cold shivers ran up and down my spine as we pushed our way through the leafy thickness, pausing every few feet, and holding our breath as we strained our eyes and ears for any sight or sound that would betray a hostile presence.

There was only silence.

A few hundred yards inland the trail came out into a spot cleared of underbrush: an Indian campsite. It was at this very place that we had left gifts for them several days before. (I must explain that we graded our gifts according to the importance of the contact. On first contact, we left only simple presents—a few paring knives, a couple of tin cans we had filled with hard corn, an empty five-gallon tin. The more valued items—a machete, an ax, sugar, or beads —we held back for a later, more complete contact.)

We rejoiced over what we saw: the natives had taken our gifts. Our first gesture of friendship had met with success. Hurriedly, we took out what we had brought along for just this purpose—an ax, some bigger knives, more cans of food. Then, concluding that we had accomplished enough for one day and that we had better not push things too far, we beat a retreat back to the river.

We let two days go by before we made another sortie to the clearing. This time our joy was even greater. Not only had the Indians taken our presents: they had left some of their own in return. Leaning down over a bare spot on the ground, we picked up a couple of hundred turtle eggs; one of their bamboo arrows, fascinatingly decorated with turkey feathers; and a crude knife with a wooden handle.

As I examined the knife more carefully, my mind filled with disturbing thoughts. Although razor sharp, the metal was curved in the middle and pitted with rust. All too plainly, it had been hammered out of a shotgun barrel. How had the savage come by that gun? And what had happened to the owner? Had he fallen a victim to one of those silent arrows? And had he been eaten afterward, which, according to rumors, was the fate of captives?

I dared not pursue these thoughts any further. In spite of them, the evidence on the whole was encouraging. At no time since we first ventured upriver had our chances of finally establishing a friendly relationship appeared brighter.

We decided to paddle a little way, hoping to come onto some of the Indians along the bank. We chose paddling for fear the sound of the outboard might frighten them back into the bush.

About a half hour later, as we rounded a curve in the river, Dave lifted his paddle and let out a hissing whisper: "There they are!"

On a narrow strip of sand along the riverbank several hundred yards ahead, I spotted four Indians. They were crouching, a posture that expressed furtiveness and fear. They seemed ready to flee back into the protection of the bush at any moment. And indeed, when they saw us heading their way, they vanished into the jungle.

We were almost abreast of the spot where they had disappeared. Dave and Jim began shouting to them to come out. No answer— only the whisper of the wind in the trees. At this point, my emotions were mixed. Fear of the unknown made me half hope they *wouldn't* come out. But I struggled hard to overcome it.

We beached the canoe on the sandbar and left more gifts. Then we pulled out into the river and waited. Still no signs of life. We were drifting with the current, so we began to paddle. We had gone about five hundred yards when Jim, glancing over his shoulder, called out,

"Hey! They've come back!"

We looked. The Nhambiguaras had come out once more and were picking up the gifts. But as we came abreast of them, they disappeared again.

By now the sun was sinking behind the trees. We were about four miles downstream from our base, so we called it quits and started home.

That evening, as we sat around under the starry sky, the cedar log crackled and spit out sparks from the fire. Dave asked, "I wonder. Should we take our guns tomorrow? Maybe we could get a duck or a turkey. Or maybe it's best if we don't carry guns right now?"

I said, "It wouldn't be too hot an idea to have the guns along if the savages are around. They'd probably figure we're out to get 'em and pump us full of arrows."

There were pros and cons to the question, and the discussion continued for some time.

I went on: "In John 18:36 it says, 'Jesus answered, My kingdom is not of this world: if my kingdom were of this world, then would my servants fight, that I should not be delivered to the Jews.' In Acts, neither Stephen nor Paul fought back or tried to kill to defend themselves. Personally, I'd rather be killed than kill and have that on my conscience all my life." We made up our minds we would follow the examples in the Word.

The following morning, Jim, Dave, and Tom set out again. I

stayed behind to guard the house. Never had I experienced a day of such overwhelming loneliness. My thoughts were with the fellows. I wondered, minute-by-minute, what might be happening to them. Nor was I free of anxiety over my own safety. We were camped on the opposite side. Uneasily, however, I remembered a place we had seen upriver where the water was so shallow the Indians could easily wade across. Every time I heard the stirring of an animal in the underbrush I jumped. Every time our dogs barked I froze.

Just before twilight, as I was stoking up the fire to cook our beans and rice, the welcome sound of voices came up from the path to the river. The fellows were back.

"Guess what!" Jim exclaimed, his eyes shining. "We made contact this afternoon." Then he went on to tell the story. "As we floated downriver, we saw about six of them, standing in the same place where we saw them yesterday. And what do you know? They signaled us to come over. We agreed I'd stay in the boat, while Tom and Dave swam to the sandbar. It was about two hundred feet."

Then Dave picked up the story: "Everything seemed to be going okay. We thought we were making real progress. It's amazing how we could understand each other without knowing the other's language. All at once, for no reason we could see, the Indians began to get jumpy. I guess they didn't entirely trust us. We knew the time had come to take off, so we did. But just before we left, we arranged—by pantomiming sleep and the angle of the sun—to meet them again at the same place at eight o'clock the next morning. We've got ourselves a date. So—when's supper ready? Boy, am I hungry!"

I didn't get much sleep that night. At daybreak we packed some more presents in case we were fortunate enough to make contact. This time it was Jim's turn to stay and guard the house. He wore a long face when he waved us good-by. He was wishing he could go along, and I knew how he felt.

It was the 6th of September, 1951. I noted it in my diary, for this could be an historic day. Going downstream was easy paddling, so I had time to think—too much time. There came to my mind Dave's description of how nervous the Nhambiguaras were at their meeting the previous afternoon. I tried to steel myself for the coming encounter. Again I found myself half hoping it wouldn't take place. I tried singing hymns in my mind. But before I could complete a single stanza, I found my thoughts gravitating to plans for self-preservation. I didn't want to die just yet. (I told myself it was because I had as yet accomplished so little of the Lord's work. The plain fact was I just didn't want to die.) In my mind, I worked out just what I would do if attacked. I would dive overboard on the far side of the canoe and swim as far as I could downstream with the current to escape the flying arrows. This was a great weakness on my part—but it was the weakness of the flesh.

Then I recalled that at home in the States, when I had embarked on this missionary career, I had told the Lord I would give my life, if need be, for Him. This resolve gave me strength. I would not go back on my word.

A long stretch of river came into view. There, on the strip of sand beside the bank, about eight Indians were waiting for us.

We pulled up slowly and beached the canoe. My heart was pounding at double time. What would they do? How would they receive us? I scarcely had a moment to speculate. They began swarming all over us, jabbering with strange, guttural noises like so many monkeys.

It was the first time I had seen any of these legendary creatures at such close range. They were all naked; I had never encountered more magnificent physical specimens. Although slightly shorter than we were, they were beautifully proportioned. With every quick, catlike movement, one could see the play of their full, developed muscles under the tawny skin. Some had "Dutch bob" haircuts across their broad foreheads, with their black hair hanging loose down their backs. Others seemed to have short, crude crewcuts, as though they had chopped the hair with some primitive cutting instrument.

They came right up and embraced us with crushing bear hugs. I noticed they were smiling broadly; not knowing what else to do, I smiled back. In fact, I smiled so long and so hard my cheek muscles ached.

Then they began feeling us all over—our hair, our eyes, our skin —as though we were alien creatures dropped from another planet. It made me uncomfortable when they started squeezing the flesh on my arms and legs, meanwhile chattering to one another— as though estimating how much meat they would get from me in a stewpot!

One of them knelt down and began fooling around with my feet. I couldn't figure out what he had in mind, until I realized he was trying to get my shoe off. When it didn't give, I surmised he must have thought it a natural part of my anatomy, for after a couple of tries he gave up.

At the same time another Indian was yanking at my left hand. I remembered then, to my regret, that I had forgotten to leave my wedding ring at home. This Indian's eye had been attracted by the glitter of the wide gold band. I pretended to co-operate with him, for I knew that at this delicate juncture of our relations, the slightest opposition could precipitate a crisis. But I did not want to lose my wedding band, either. So while I pretended to help him, I kept my finger bent slightly, making it impossible for him to budge it past the knuckle. He finally gave up.

I had scarcely solved this touchy situation when a new one presented itself. A squat, stalwart Indian took a stance immediately in front of me, smiled, thrust a forefinger into my mouth, and began probing around. This filled me with alarm, for I had false teeth. It crossed my mind that if he found out they were loose and could take them out, he would be so enchanted with the discovery that he would make off with them and I would never see them again. I needed my teeth badly to chew the tough meat that formed such an essential ingredient of our diet.

He was still probing. He might make his unfortunate discovery at any moment. There was only one thing to do. I took a chance and bit his finger as hard as I could. The smile faded from his face, giving way to a look of pain and angry surprise. Immediately I doubled over, laughing as hard as I could to get across that that was my idea of a rough joke. The tactic seemed to bewilder him completely. He turned away from me and began investigating Tom.

I was left alone for a moment. My glance wandered off beyond the knot of playful, jabbering Indians among us to the impenetrable wall of jungle beyond the sandbar. A shiver ran up my spine. The broad leaves swayed with a motion not caused by wind. I was certain I saw pairs of black beady eyes fixed upon us. I had the feeling that while these eight or so had come out to meet us, back there, under cover, scores of savages with bows and arrows were just waiting for us to make one gesture that looked hostile to them. This time we had no guns. We had left them behind purposely so as to avoid any cause for alarm. We were completely at their mercy. It behooved us to "take it" and be on our best behavior.

Another thing bothered me. No one gave any orders. None had any distinctive mark of authority either in bearing or in decoration. This could mean only that among those who had come out to meet us, none was the chief. So every man was on his own, responsible to no one but himself, free to follow his impulse.

Suddenly, there came a tremendous yank at my head from behind. It nearly pulled me over, and I felt an excruciating pain. Turning, I saw a husky savage grinning at me triumphantly. In his hand he held a sizable wad of my blondish hair. My stage smile must have vanished into a rather odd expression of surprise and pain. But when I saw how intently the Indian was studying my face, watching for my reaction, I quickly forced my tired muscles back into a smile. This must have had the desired effect, for—as if to show that it was all in good clean fun—the Indian went over to one of his pals and tried to pull out a similar wad of thick black hair. His must have been more firmly rooted than mine because it did not yield. Not to be thwarted so easily, the jolly prankster pulled the hapless one's head close to his mouth and began chewing it off—hair by hair, as a woman bites off threads.

We were wondering how long this horseplay would go on. Finally, two of them drew away from us and huddled together, whispering and casting suspicious looks in our direction. We did not like this turn of events. In sign language, we explained we must leave and would be back at four o'clock. Then, with all seemly haste, we paddled away upriver.

At the appointed hour we returned. We had no idea what to expect. A larger group was standing there awaiting us; we saw many faces we had not seen before. This time, they made no effort to inspect us. The curiosity of the new ones among them had probably been satisfied by what the others told them.

We hastened to present our gifts before they could start any more horseplay. We met them halfway on the strand. We had some bags of sugar and "farina," a coarse cereal made from yucca, which looks a little like Grapenuts. They just stared at it warily. We caught on and each ate some of it ourselves to show we had no intention of poisoning them. After that they fell upon it greedily.

Since the atmosphere was friendly and relaxed, Dave brought out a pad of paper and a pencil and got ready to write down their language sounds.

Flying around overhead were several dun-colored river birds resembling sea gulls, except they were smaller, and had straight beaks. I pointed to one and looked questioningly at the nearest Indian. He made a sound in his language and I wrote it down phonetically. Then, looking at the marks, I tried to pronounce the sound he had made. This really mystified him: he thought the marks on the paper were talking. Others insisted on making marks on the paper themselves. Then they would stand back and wait for the marks to talk. When nothing happened, they showed their disappointment.

From our first efforts it was becoming clear that what Don Juan had told us was true: we were up against one of the most complicated languages in the world, one that had probably existed for thousands of years and never been written down. This was only one job we would have to accomplish before we could begin explaining the Gospel to them. Many of the sounds they uttered had no counterparts in English or Spanish. They involved using the throat and the lips in an entirely different way.

On the other hand, we had but to speak a sentence in English once, and they could repeat it right back to us without missing a syllable. We felt rather foolish. In spite of their aboriginal customs, these were obviously a highly intelligent people. Their minds must have been honed to remarkable sharpness over the centuries in their struggles to survive against nature, other tribes, and the marauding white man. Given the advantages of training and education, they would undoubtedly be able to hold their own anywhere in the world. This discovery made us all the more eager to befriend and convert them. They seemed really friendly toward us—at ease and free of suspicion.

But now we began to be afflicted by the discomforts of nature. Two hours had gone by. We had never remained so long with them before. It was hot out on the sandbar, but we didn't as yet dare venture into the jungle with our hosts to escape the sun. As we were sweating, thousands of gnats settled down on us, leaving annoying little red welts wherever they stung.

Once again we took our leave, saying in sign language we would be back tomorrow. Our friends seemed genuinely sorry to see us go. Our hearts were light. Not since we had set out to contact the Nhambiguaras had we felt so free from fear and so hopeful that someday we would be able to achieve our goal.

As we neared a bend, we gave a last look back. The Indians were raising their legs and slapping at them in what looked at first like a ritual dance. Then we realized the truth. They were merely carrying on the fight from which we had fled—the ceaseless war with the gnats!

That evening we were full of plans for our next contact. But during the night the wind shifted, bringing with it cold, intermittent rain and chilly gusts from the south. In the next twenty days there were only four contacts, and even those were sporadic and unsatisfactory. Evidently the Nhambiguaras, unprotected against the elements, did not like to leave their huts when the weather turned damp and cold.

One really worrisome incident occurred during this interval. It happened when Dave and Tom had taken the canoe for a couple of days' hunting upriver. Tom heard a rustling which he took to indicate the presence of wild pigs. Gun in hand, he scrambled up the bank. Just as he reached the top, he heard a thud in a tree trunk close to his ear. He turned to see an arrow, still quivering, which had struck not three inches from his head. He made it to the bottom of the embankment in about two jumps.

Tom and Dave were on their way back from upriver when a dozen or so Indians with bows in their hands came running up to them on the edge of the riverbank, and started jabbering fiercely. They did not recognize these as any they had seen before. Just then another Indian appeared and spoke to the others in a low, calm voice. Immediately, they quieted down; Tom and Dave brought out their gifts and tranquillity returned.

For several nights afterward this constituted the Number One topic of conversation at our campfire bull sessions. Had the Indians seen him climbing the bank with his gun and thought he was on his way to attack them?

At our camp at Paredon, we were kept awake on a number of occasions by the insistent barking of our dogs. The morning after the first occurrence, we checked the surrounding muddy areas. Strange footprints were everywhere. Then we remembered something the rubber hunters had told us: if the Indians come around a camp at night, it is either to steal or to kill.

On another morning following a sleepless night, we heard the dogs barking and went out to see what was going on. A hundred and fifty feet from the house we stumbled onto six Indians gliding silently through the jungle underbrush. One of them gave a call. Immediately the whole area was alive with answering calls. Then we knew there were many, many more of them lurking where our eyes could not penetrate.

We smiled and made friendly gestures to those we could see, eventually motioning to them to follow us back to the house. About a dozen of them came and they all sat down in a row on a log. We had never entertained them at our own camp before, and we were curious to see their reactions to our ways. I watched their faces intently as I poured some kerosene on the wood. To them kerosene was water; they must have wondered why I was doing it. Then, when I touched a match to it and the "water" caught fire, their eyes popped. Chattering together like magpies, they pointed incredulously, crowded around, and insisted on inspecting our matches, those mysterious sticks which had performed such magic. These they passed around. But they still did not seem to understand what had happened.

The matches kept them occupied until dinner was ready. We gave them some fish we had caught the night before to roast in the fire. Soon we had a kettle full of rice and chopped corned beef mixed in, boiling away. A couple of the Indians were impatient and snatched out the fish. They were too raw to be pulled apart. That didn't make any difference. One of them laid the fish on the ground and was able, by putting his foot on half of it, to tear it apart with two hands. He tossed a piece to me and it fell short. Picking it up, I tried to get off what dirt I could. Again asking the Lord to help me keep it down, I began chewing away on it.

Roasted bananas were cleaner eating. We peeled off the thick burned skin and enjoyed the sweet soft texture.

When the rice was set aside to cool off, the Indians again became impatient. They stuck their fingers in to get some, then let out a howl because it was steaming hot. But eventually they cleaned it all up. We ate with our fingers, too, so as not to lose our spoons to them.

Later that evening they suddenly slipped off into the jungle and vanished.

9

Commando Wives

Two weeks later, after one of the rare contacts during the twenty-day period, we were paddling back across the river to have our noonday dinner when we heard the sound of the diesel approaching from downriver. Jim and I were excited, for we were sure there would be letters from our wives, whom we had not seen in three months.

After eating, we went down to the riverbank. We were waiting there when the bell rang for a landing. The mail boat drew up; the crewmen put the well-worn gangplank overside, and began coming ashore. Both of our wives had written. We tore open the envelopes and felt warmed and relieved as we read. They were anxious to join us as soon as we felt it was safe enough.

But we faced a new situation. The Indians, waiting on the far bank for our return, had been seen by the crewmen, who were now in a high state of excitement. For years they had heard and repeated lurid, bloodcurdling tales of the Nhambiguaras. Many of the men had never had a good look at the Indians, who remained for them only legendary phantoms, living in concealment in the bush.

96

Bruce, Edith, and three-year-old Connie Porterfield with a catch of catfish near their lonely camp at Paredon, in the heart of the Bolivian jungle where first contact with the savage Nhambiguara Indians was made.

In the market place at Cochabamba, Indian women in white derby hats display their wares and barter vigorously. Before setting out for tribal territory, the Porterfields had to wait months in this city for vital supplies and household goods to arrive. (Chapter 2)

Marauding army ants swept through the Porterfields' home in Cafetal, killing and carrying away every living thing in their path (Chapter 5). At all jungle outposts, the kitchen (right) must be a separate structure, for soot and smoke from primitive wood stoves blacken everything.

An old flat-bottomed riverboat carried the Porterfields 500 miles up the Rio Guaporé to the mission outpost at Cafetal, jungle headquarters for the effort to reach the Nhambiguara tribe. (Chapter 4)

Missionary Dave Yarwood became friendly with the Nhambiguara savages who later killed him in a sudden, unexplained attack. Here he poses with two tribesmen on the sandbar where pioneering contacts were made. (Chapter 8)

Jim Ostewig and other missionaries tried to write down the sounds they could catch when the Nhambiguaras spoke. The Indians thought the pencil was magic; here one tries to make "marks that talk." Another tribesman wears the sweater Bruce gave him. (Chapter 8)

Outwardly friendly, the Nhambiguaras were also wary and prone to sudden violence. This smiling tribesman is proud of his goatee, a rarity in the usually clean-shaven tribe. (Chapter 8)

Bruce sets out bananas, knives, and tin cans on the sandbar, hoping the gifts will attract the Nhambiguaras to the meeting place for another chance to make friends and pave the way for the Gospel. (Chapter 9)

When crewmen from the riverboat handed out magazines and approached their womenfolk, the Nhambiguaras responded with a hostility that may have led to the later murder of Dave Yarwood (right). See Chapter 9.

...bber hunters were the only outsiders missionaries found when they arrived in ...e Bolivian jungle. Here an Indian worker heats the liquid rubbermilk over an ...en until it coagulates on the pole into a huge ball for shipping downriver to port ...arkets. (Chapter 11)

Poling through the dense swamp above the Rio Terebinto is a perilous and backbreaking task. Mysterious vines in the tall grass temporarily paralyzed some of the missionaries on the way to a new camp in Macurapi Indian territory. Seen over Ewart Sadler's shoulder are (left to right) Dorothy Abbey, the children, Lyle Stuart, a Bolivian guide, and Wilbur Abbey. (Chapter 11)

Lyle Stuart guns the outboard motor to plow through thick undergrowth on the Rio Terebinto; up front, Dorothy and Lila use dishpans to shield themselves from sharp branches. (Chapter 11)

aluminum boat could be unloaded and lifted r logs blocking the river; the much heavier oe had to be emptied, submerged, and pushed erneath. (Chapter 11)

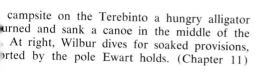

campsite on the Terebinto a hungry alligator urned and sank a canoe in the middle of the . At right, Wilbur dives for soaked provisions, rted by the pole Ewart holds. (Chapter 11)

The torn clothing of Ewart Sadler and Dorothy Abbey shows the toll taken by thorns and branches on the long journey through the river and swamp. (Chapter 11)

At their camp beyond the swa. Dorothy cooks over an open while Macurapi women and c dren look on. Weeks passed be dwellings with mud-brick sto could be completed at this isola jungle outpost. (Chapter 11)

Dorothy Abbey and Lila Sharp write their last letters home before their camp is cut off from the outside world by the dry season. A few days later the Porterfields and Ewart Sadler left for other posts; ten months would pass before the rains would fill the swamp and restore the lifeline of communication and supply. (Chapter 11)

Months later, Bruce fights his way back through the swamp with emergency supplies for the Abbeys and Sharps. (Chapter 12)

New challenge: at Todos Santos, five missionaries set out for the jungle to try to head off a war between Bolivian farmers and the savage Yuqui tribe. Left to right: Don Hay, Wayne Gill, Bob Wilhelmson, Les Foster, and Bruce Porterfield. (Chapter 13)

In the heart of dangerous Yuqui territory, the missionaries built a stronghouse in a clearing. When wary tribesmen arrived for a meeting by crossing the creek on the log visible at left, Bruce concealed himself under the eaves at the back of the building and took the pictures which appear on the following three pages. (Chapter 14)

During the tense moments of talk with the tribe, the missionaries tried to hide
their nervousness with smiles. Left to right: a Yuqui youngster, Les Foster, a
warrior, the chief's wife (with shaved scalp), Harold Rainey, the Yuqui chief,
Hudson Birkett, Chuck Johnson, and Dick Strickler. (Chapter 14)

Missionaries try to get across their message of friendship and peace to stone-a
savages. The Yuqui chief is in the foreground; the warrior at his right bears t
scar of a bullet wound from the war with the farmers. (Chapter 14)

Yuqui tribesman whirled and looked up when he heard a click from Bruce's
ra. Moments later he climbed up and discovered the hiding place, bringing the
onaries' peace mission close to disaster. (Chapter 14)

Missionaries have built this armored boat as their floating headquarters in the latest effort to reach the Yuquis and open the way for the message of the Gospel. (Chapter 15)

"My desire in writing this book has been to portray not only the missionary struggles, his heartbreaks, emotions, and hopes, but also the strength of his convictions, which lead him to press on, faithful to his promises to God even unto death."

Several crewmen demanded point blank that we take them along on our contacts. Others, more cautious, asked us how dangerous we thought it would be. We did not answer them at once, for we were plagued by doubts.

What we had learned earlier of these men and of their background, and of their relations to the Indians, gave us concern. They worked the mail boats not as a permanent job but usually for only a trip or two, as a means of getting upcountry or back again. They were a restless, roving lot, bent chiefly on realizing their dreams of sudden riches. Many of them had come from the larger cities of eastern Brazil. The jungle lured them like a magnet. It abounded with incredible legends of buried treasure, of hidden hoards of gold, of rough diamonds as big as the end of one's forefinger, of Indians who went around with ancient beaten-gold ornaments believed to be handed down from the Incas. No substance was ever found to support these stories; but they were repeated often enough and with enough conviction to keep the adventurers forever on the search.

Thus their overwhelming desire to make contact with the Indians. The motives, though quite different from our own, were nevertheless impelling. Now that they had seen the savages with their own eyes, the crewmen's appetites were whetted.

We missionaries knew only too well the long history of bloodshed and killings on both sides. If the slightest thing went wrong, all our patient work would go for naught. Furthermore, if this happened, we, along with the nationals, stood a good chance of being killed. Yet, we were in no position to refuse. We were guests in their country. We had no authority over them. They or others like them had extended us many kindnesses and courtesies. We depended on the mail boat for our supplies. They told us they wanted only to take some presents to the Indians.

So, much against our better judgment, and with many cautionary admonitions to be on their best behavior, we agreed to take three of them across with us in our canoe.

The Nhambiguaras, who were waiting in the clearing under the trees, regarded us warily as we approached with strangers. They were poised as though ready to flee. But Dave waved to them and called out in a friendly voice. That seemed to reassure them, for they remained as we beached our canoe.

Everything went well at first. The rivermen, overawed at being face to face with these wild creatures of the jungle, were on their best behavior. They hung back, letting us make the approaches.

Little by little the crewmen gained confidence. They brought presents from the dugout, which put our modest gifts to shame, including such items as large amounts of sugar and rice, clothes, knives, and machetes. The Indians, examining and exclaiming over each new present, were like delighted children.

To our dismay, we saw that the rivermen were taking over the contact. Imitating us, they tried to communicate in sign language and guttural sounds. The atmosphere, on the surface at least, was still friendly and relaxed. Then they made signs to the Indians to bring out their wives and children, who during our contacts always stayed half hidden about a hundred feet back in the jungle. We had often remarked that the Indians still suspected us, for they never allowed their women and children to come out to where we were. The overtures of the nationals now gave the Indians some grounds for their suspicion. And when the rivermen began to make signs to the Indian women who were peering through the under-brush, inviting them to cross the river and inspect the mail boat, the whole atmosphere changed in an instant. Some of the Indian men gathered into a tight group, whispering. They looked our way, their faces contorted in rage.

I could understand their mistrust. Had they not the memories of times long past when their women were stolen by rubber hunters, never to be seen again? Quite naturally, they feared their wives might be kidnaped.

One of the Indian men walked away. As I watched, he reached the women and children and signaled them to follow him.

"We better get these fellows out of here before there's trouble," I said.

David uttered a sharp warning. I wouldn't have been surprised had arrows come flying at us from the jungle. We hurried our guests into the canoe.

On the return trip, we reproached the rivermen for their conduct. We might as well have saved our breath, for they merely laughed at us. They considered their first contact a success. Nothing overt had happened. Their chief impression was the pleasure of the Indians over receiving their gifts. They spoke happily of making further contacts five days from now on their return trip from Matto Grosso. They began to dream the riverman's dream of finding Indian villages filled with gold ornaments and buried treasure.

"I've been to one of their villages," I said to them. "Believe me, there's nothing there. They really live poor."

They smiled skeptically at me, as though convinced I was keeping my secrets to myself.

Shortly after we got back, they went aboard the mail boat. For once, we were glad to see it disappear upriver.

We saw trouble ahead. For hours afterward, Jim, Dave, and I talked of nothing else. Tom was quiet throughout, with a solemn, intent expression.

As nightfall settled upon us, the conversation continued. We got a fire going. Plainly, we were disturbed. Whenever one finished saying something, another would begin immediately.

"Listen fellows," Tom said finally. "There's only one thing to do. I'm going up to Matto Grosso on the next boat."

"What's the idea?" Jim wanted to know.

"I'm going to go see the provincial governor and get an order restraining these characters from making any further contact with the Indians in areas where we're working."

We were quiet. The notion had never occurred to us.

"You mean kind of an injunction?" Jim inquired.

Tom nodded. "That's right: an injunction."

"What makes you think he'll give it to you?" Dave demanded.

Tom had his answer ready. "You know very well that if anything like this happens again, it's going to end in bloodshed. Then the men going through this area will continue fighting these Indians for years and years. On the other hand, if we're allowed to keep on by ourselves, maybe we can win their friendship and establish a peace that could last a long time. We've got too much at stake to run any more risks. I bet I can make the governor see things our way."

All of us agreed to the wisdom of his plan.

"I've got another idea that may help save this situation," I said.

"Just a minute, Bruce. Before you start I'll get the coffeepot on," Dave said. We laughed: how well Dave liked his coffee was a standing joke. He dug out a few hot coals and set the coffeepot on them.

"What would you guys think of bringing Helen and Edith and the kids up here to stay with us?" I asked.

"Man, you crazy?" Dave said. "You never know but what those Indians might want to haul off *your* wives and children."

"Maybe," I answered. His thoughts shook me, but I continued. "If these Indians see that Jim and I have families, then they'll know that we have no ulterior motives of wanting *their* women and children. It might break down this barrier of fear. You can see how they still mistrust our motives. Don't forget—on all these contacts we've made with them, they never have allowed their wives and children to come out. If their suspicion grows, we may all end up in their soup kettle."

Everybody was quiet again. The croaking bullfrogs down by the river were having a discussion of their own. Our two dogs slept peacefully.

"You might have something there, Bruce," Dave said at last. "As far as I can tell—except for the incident this afternoon—our relations with the Indians are good and getting better. I don't see any harm in bringing your families. In fact, their presence might be a great help to us. What do you think, Jim?"

"I'd been thinking the same thing," said Jim. "When the boat comes back in a few days, someone has to go down and get more supplies from Cafetal. That would be the time to bring our wives up—if we're convinced it's safe. Tom could go on up to Matto Grosso on the same boat."

I was elected to go downriver to Cafetal. After finishing our coffee we had our devotions and went to bed.

For a long time I couldn't sleep. Dave's words concerning the possibility of our wives and children being kidnaped struck terror into my heart. I pictured Edith and Connie captured (Brian was in Cochabamba at our mission school), and also pictured my desperate planning and struggling for months in an effort to get them back. I thought, "Am I being presumptuous in saying I'll trust the Lord to protect them? Or should I use the common sense God gives us and not bring them?" Yet common sense reasoned, too, that it *was* best to bring them. Such conflict! I tossed on my mattress. "Lord," I prayed, "take this fear out of my heart."

It was great to be back in Cafetal and to see Edith and Connie. I reveled in the luxury of sleeping in a real bed again. When I learned we would have to remain there several days, waiting for the mail boat to come up from Guajara Mirim, it didn't bother me in the least. But Edith and Helen and even little Connie, who was now three, were eager to get going. They were looking forward to camping out as a great adventure. After all, they'd had to endure the monotony of daily life in this Bolivian village, whereas we were at least buoyed up by the fascination of our developing contacts with the Nhambiguaras.

At last, far off in the distance, the *thump-thump-thump* of the diesel told us the mail boat would soon be here. We were ready and waiting at the landing. Beside us were stacks of boxes containing staple food supplies, including plenty of powdered milk for the children, gifts for the Indians, and tins of gasoline. Our dugout, which the mail boat had towed down to Cafetal, would also be towed again partly loaded back up to Paredon. This was customary; four or five of them usually bobbed behind the mail boat on every trip.

Helen and Edith were keyed up over the prospect of seeing new faces and new places. We were told that because of the difficulties of navigating during the dry season, the journey to Paredon would take about four days, instead of the usual three. But nobody minded very much. Helen and Edith seemed to have forgotten altogether the hardships endured on the way upriver to Cafetal.

After the boat docked and we boarded, I strung up the jungle hammocks. Since we were a little crowded, Helen decided to have the baby sleep with her. The nights on the river are damp and very cool.

Our progress was slow, for the pilot had to nose his way cautiously around logs, rocks, and sandbars. But the time passed quickly. Our journey became a kind of social excursion. We made friends with the other passengers, mostly Bolivian rubber workers on their way back to the jungle. Wherever people were clustered along the bank, the boat would stop—sometimes to take on or discharge passengers or cargo, sometimes just to barter for turtle eggs or wild meat. I was hardly aware of the stink of the hides any more, or even of the pounding diesel which had so disturbed our sleep at first.

We came to the last evening of our trip. According to our calculations, we should reach our camp at Paredon around midnight. We were expecting the fellows to be down at the landing with their flashlights to meet us. Shortly after dark, Edith and Helen put the youngsters to sleep in their hammocks. Then we sat around on the bags for awhile, talking.

About nine o'clock it began to grow chilly. The women lay in their hammocks for warmth and rest, even if they couldn't sleep. Helen showed us how she had learned to wad the blanket around the baby and herself to keep warm.

I stretched out right there on some bags of rice. I did not close my eyes. All my thoughts were of Jim, Dave, and Tom at Paredon. I wondered what they had been doing in the two weeks since I left and whether they had made any fresh contacts. My thoughts drifted away. Before I knew it, I fell asleep.

I have no idea how much later it was when I jerked awake by

an awful jolt, followed by a muffled crash. Still half asleep, I jumped up. Water was rushing around my legs. The boat tilted. We were sinking.

My dulled senses tried to grasp this fact. Then I heard Helen's voice nearby cry out in panic.

"Help me! Help me! I can't get out of this hammock."

It was almost pitch black. Only a faint glimmer from a lantern on the diesel boat alongside filtered now and then through the palm-thatched roof of our boat, making pale, drifting shafts of light.

I groped my way toward Helen's cry. "It's okay!" I called with hearty assurance I did not feel. "I'll be right with you."

I reached the hammock. The water was coming up fast. It was almost up to where she lay with the baby. I probed with my feet to find something solid beneath me. The boat had listed so by now that I kept slipping and sliding and could hardly stand erect.

With my hands I could feel Helen struggling and thrashing to free the baby and herself. I grabbed for the blankets. I could not pull them loose: she had wadded them in all too well. The best I could do, by pressing upward with all my strength, was to hold Helen and the baby, with my outstretched arms, inches above the rising water.

Something hit me and I went under. Helen cried out. I got to my feet again just in time to see a big gasoline drum swim by. Once more I seized hold of the hammock. I did not know when I might be knocked down again—and perhaps not be able to get up next time.

Another shape floated by: a large box. Blankets for our stay up-river!

I do not know how long I stood there with my arms aching, holding up the hammock while also scrambling to keep some kind of foothold on the slippery planking. Then I took heart: Helen had managed to free her arms. But my strength was ebbing fast.

Only a few feet away was the diesel boat lashed alongside, a haven of safety—if only we could reach it. The palm-leafed roof parted, letting in a little light. I saw a head and shoulders. In Portuguese, a gruff voice said, "Here—hand the baby to me."

I took the child from Helen's arms and passed her over. The man's head and shoulders reappeared. With his help, I freed Helen and handed her over also.

Finally, I climbed over into the diesel boat. Standing there, in the faint light of the lantern, were Edith and Connie. They were shivering but they were safe. I let out a sob of joy and thanks to the Lord.

Edith stepped forward and threw her arms around me. "Oh, thank God you're safe," she cried. "I didn't know what had become of you. I didn't see you anywhere."

One by one, all the passengers were accounted for. The diesel engine began to chug. Slowly, it pulled the sunken mail boat into shallow waters along the riverbank.

We gathered on the embankment. It was about ten o'clock at night. What a miserable, shivering bedraggled lot! We had no way of knowing how many of our supplies had been washed away. But at this point we didn't care. We were thankful our lives had been spared. A passage from Isaiah (43:2) flashed into my mind: "When thou passest through the waters, I will be with thee; and through the rivers, they shall not overflow thee. . . ."

About two o'clock in the morning the captain came over to where we were still standing around, to explain that the boat had hit only a submerged sandbar. It was not damaged fatally. As soon as morning came, he said, the crew would try to get going again and would attempt to salvage the lost cargo. In the meantime, there was nothing to be done. None of us looked forward to the prospect of shivering there for the rest of the night.

I struck up a conversation with a man standing next to me in the dark. A young and energetic Bolivian rubber worker, he seemed less stunned by the accident than most of the others. I told him how worried we were that the children might catch cold. I explained what a discouraging setback it was for this to have happened when we were only three or four hours from our destination. I showed him our canoe, tied up on the shore behind the sunken ship. He nodded sympathetically, indicating his own smaller dugout. He was silent for a bit.

When he spoke again, his voice was vigorous. "I've still got my outboard motor," he said. "You have the big canoe. Why not attach my motor to your dugout and we'll go upriver together to your camp? When the mail boat's running again, I can have it stop for me and continue my trip."

The idea appealed to me. But I had to weigh the hazards of his trying to navigate that tricky river by night. I talked it over with Helen and Edith. We agreed it was better than standing around for the rest of the night, wet, cold, and miserable.

Wrapping ourselves in our wet blankets, which gave a minimum of protection against the chilly river breezes, we took off. There were six of us. Edith and I sat on some boxes in the middle; the Bolivian sat in the stern, steering, his eyes boring into the darkness ahead. We were no more than a few inches above the water. Every time we changed direction at all, we shipped water. Edith and I bailed away almost steadily.

I wished we could all sing hymns to keep up our spirits. But we could not have made ourselves heard above the noise of the outboard; besides, our teeth were chattering so, we could not have got the words out. So I sang one of my old favorites in my mind.

> Never a day so dreary, never a night so long
> But the soul that is trusting Jesus will
> somewhere find a song.

> Wonderful, wonderful Jesus
> In the heart He implanteth a song.
> A song of deliverance, of courage,
> of strength
> In my heart He implanteth a song.

The night, though cold, was clear. Pale stars shed just enough light to reveal the sinister shapes in the river, but barely enough for us to avoid them. We set our course primarily by the ragged line of trees against the sky.

It was almost sunrise when we were able to pick out the familiar high rust-red cliff of Paredon. Jim, Tom, and Dave were down at the landing to welcome us, and to tell us how worried they had been. They had been listening to the sound of the diesel, which carries as far as twenty miles in the jungle, then, upon hearing it stop, couldn't imagine what had happened.

As we climbed the hill to the house, we told them the story. Dave got a fire going and put some coffee on. Jim laid out some dry clothes for Helen and Edith and a dry blanket for the children, then went out to bring some supplies from the boat. The women hung their dresses out on the line to dry. But there was no time to take things easy. No more than half an hour after we had arrived, Jim came running in to tell us that a bunch of Nhambiguaras had appeared just across the river. They were making signs for us to go over. I learned this was the first important contact since I had left, and we didn't want to miss it. We went outside.

Edith and Helen, eager, too, for their first sight of the stone-age men, came running out to go with us. They had quite forgotten the clothes they wore—Jim and Tom's dry trousers and shirts. I hesitated a minute. What would the Indians think at seeing our wives dressed like us? Would they attempt to molest them? No, I thought, I must commit their lives into the hands of the Lord, trusting that their presence would break down the barriers of fear and suspicion.

And so, at the first sight of our wives, an event on which we had counted so much, the Indians would see them dressed like men! We entered the dugout and paddled across the river. We took Connie also. Tom, doing last-minute packing to go upriver on the boat to Matto Grosso, stayed behind and looked after the Ostewigs' baby. The Indian men—about fifteen of them—waved to us from shore. Again I glimpsed the women and children, half hidden in the jungle underbrush. This time they were craning their necks for a look at Helen, Edith, and Connie.

We landed and immediately absorbed ourselves in the all-important first moments of the contact. I noticed at once that the chief still hadn't come out. What significance did that have?

I chanced to glance in the direction of the Indian women. My heart sank. There was Connie, about halfway between us and the Indian women and children, who were a hundred feet back from where we stood, and she was making a beeline toward them. It was too late to stop her. I didn't want to show fear or to alarm the Indians by running after her—which meant running toward their women. Connie disappeared into the jungle and emerged a moment later, leading a couple of small Indian children by the hand. Then several women, all as naked as the day they were born, came out after their children. Edith and Helen began to make a fuss over the Indian children, which caused their mothers to smile. Then, in a combination of sign language and verbal sounds, our wives attempted to communicate with them, just as we were doing with the men. Thanks to Connie, the gathering took on the friendly atmosphere of a church social.

Now that the Nhambiguaras knew we had wives and children of our own, they were evidently losing their fears that we would kidnap theirs. This marked a great step forward in our relations with them.

But later in the morning the boat crew would be along. The crew would see the Indian women, which spelled almost certain trouble. In sign language, we warned the Indians to make their wives and children go back into hiding when they heard the boat coming. The Indian men, with repeated gestures and nods, indicated their agreement.

The first contact with the women went very well. It took quite awhile for the Indian women to tell in sign language about their children, to explain the reason for certain scars, and to point out the differences between our women and themselves.

In a few hours we heard the boat in the distance. Again we warned the natives to make their wives go away. They did. When the boat pulled up to our landing, we were glad to see that several of our boxes had been recovered. As before, the crew members wanted to approach the Indians. Tom restrained them sharply. They were persistent and went across in the mail boat.

When the crew began handing out gifts to the Nhambiguara men, six of the Indian women rushed out to receive some also. The situation grew tense, so we warned the rivermen to get going if they didn't want to be killed. Reluctantly, they returned to our landing.

We followed after them. "Now I know I've got to go to Matto Grosso," Tom said as he climbed aboard the mail boat with his old battered suitcase. "Things will keep getting worse unless we do something quick."

"The Lord help you to get that injunction," I said.

While Tom was gone, we had a number of friendly contacts with the Nhambiguaras, which included the wives and children all meeting together. They continued to gain confidence in us. Once, on a Sunday, as we approached the group in the boat, we noticed that the women, although as bare as plucked birds, wore long, heavy necklaces.

"Isn't that just like women," I chuckled, "to get all decked out in their Sunday best?"

From a distance some of their ornaments flashed yellow in the sun. Perhaps, I reflected, it was just such glimpses that had started the rumor among the rubber workers and other adventurers that the Indians possessed priceless ornaments of gold.

Helen and Edith wanted to give the decorations closer scrutiny. The Indian women seemed delighted at this, and displayed them with pride. Suddenly, Edith called me over. "Come here, honey, I want you to see these."

When I studied the necklaces carefully, I saw they consisted entirely of buttons. They were strung on a cord common among the Indians—one they weave from fibers of kapoc that grows wild in the jungle. Some of them were ordinary mother-of-pearl—shirt buttons, perhaps. The ones that had shone like gold were actually brass. I peered at one, observing it closely. It was quite old and worn almost smooth. But the traces of English letters were still barely visible—the remnants of what might have been *Oshkosh* or *Sheboygan*.

My blood ran cold. This was the kind of metal button formerly worn to hold up overalls. A grisly thought passed through my mind: could these have once been worn by the three missionaries who died here in 1925?

Now my eye lit on some larger buttons, also old and worn, but bearing traces of quite a different design. These were unmistakably buttons of the kind worn on army uniforms in World War I. I thought of the British explorer, Colonel Fawcett. The photographs I had seen of him and his men showed them wearing such uniforms. Could this be a clue as to how he had met his end? He had disappeared in this very area, while fixing the boundary between Bolivia and Brazil. Far up the Rio Verde, I had once seen a cement marker that I guessed he had placed there.

I glanced around me at the smiling, chattering faces. Were these harmless-looking baubles evidence of their rumored cannibalism? Not daring to let my imagination roam further, I drew out my pencil and pad and diverted myself by trying once more to write down some of their language sounds.

Another day we had an experience which put our zeal as missionaries to the test. Leaving Helen and Edith at camp with the children, Dave, Jim, and I went out to make contact in the shaded clearing. The Indians, still showing an increasing friendliness, always made a point of bringing us unusual gifts. Long before they reached us, we could tell by the eager, pleased expressions on their wide, brown faces that they had prepared a particular surprise this time.

A short, muscular fellow ran ahead of the others, grinning broadly. He held a basket before us invitingly. Then we saw what it contained: about a hundred round, fat, white worms.

"They look like maggots," I murmured, feeling myself turn green.

"Don't think so," replied Jim in a low voice. "They look like the larvae of the big black hornets."

The Indian was urging us to try some.

"If that's what they are," Jim added in a low voice, "they've gone through quite an ordeal to get them. They run the risk of being painfully stung. Frederico told me than an Indian will go straight up to a big hornet's nest very slowly and scratch at it with his fingers until all the hornets are out and flying all around him. Then he'll slowly break off the limb with the nest on it and walk away. If he handles himself right, he's okay. Even if the hornets land on him, they won't sting him. Unless he makes a sudden move. Then they'll give it to him good."

This realization made me look at the larvae with a new eye. Still, I didn't know if I could bring myself to swallow one. The Indian, upon noticing my hesitation, flipped one into his own mouth. Then he tried to convey to me by his expression what a delicacy it was. Quite a few Indians had gathered around us by now to watch. It was up to us to make the next move.

"What'll we do?" I asked helplessly.

Dave had an inspiration. "Tell you what," he said in his low, deep voice. "We'll each eat one. Then we'll make the generous gesture of giving the rest back to them. If they took all that trouble to get them, our friends might just appreciate having them."

A dozen pairs of eyes—all so black that one couldn't tell where the pupil left off and the iris began—were fixed on us. Their intentness belied the smiles on their lips. We held out our hands in turn, and each helped ourselves to a worm. I popped mine into my mouth and downed it at one gulp. Out of the corner of my eye, I saw to my amazement that Jim and Dave were actually eating theirs.

Now we quickly offered the basket to the Nhambiguaras. To our immense relief, they expressed their joy at having it back. We made every effort to conceal how pleased we really were at their reaction. I had a hard time keeping mine down. Just then, crawling on a leaf nearby, I spotted some big, fuzzy caterpillars. Since the direction of their gastronomic interest was now all too plain, I was afraid that if the Indians saw the caterpillars, they would offer them to us. I would have to refuse—regardless of the consequences.

I grabbed a caterpillar and held it out to the nearest Indian. He swallowed it, fuzz and all, smiling his appreciation. Then, lest he find one in his turn and bring it to me, I snatched every caterpillar in sight and treated one Indian after another. Highly pleased, they were also diverted from any further attempts to give us more larvae.

As the Nhambiguaras continued to lose their suspicions, our meetings with them grew more satisfactory. Once they volunteered to sing for us. Sitting around in a semicircle on the sandbar, they launched forth into a tribal chant. They sang entirely in a minor key, with a strange monotony that sounded almost oriental. A hush came over the river. Even the birds seemed to have stopped to listen. After every few verses the Indians would stop, let out their breath in a hissing sound, and make a sweeping motion with their hands, as though driving off all evil spirits. Then they would resume their monotonous chant. The effect on us was curiously eerie and depressing. The evil spirits seemed all too near.

We were making real progress in our language studies. At first we concentrated on nouns. We would point to birds, trees, parts of the body, then write down what sounds they gave us. The words for "round, flat, colored" stones marked the start of learning the adjectives. For action verbs, we would do all kinds of crazy things, such as hitting each other, jumping, running, and throwing. For the sentences "I hit him" or "He hit me," we would go into action again to learn pronouns and the position of the subject and object of the verb. We were only beginning, we knew, for it takes many months, even years, to compile the necessary vocabulary for the eventual imparting of the Gospel message.

One evening the Ostewigs, Dave, and I were sitting around the campfire. Amber sparks flew upward from the burning cedar log like a Fourth-of-July set piece. Edith came out of the house where she had been making up our bed. "We're almost down to the bare boards," she said with a laugh. "Another night or two and we'll make it." Some time ago, Edith and I had hit on the idea of using our bags of dried corn and beans as a mattress. Her comment meant that once more we faced a familiar situation: our food supplies were dwindling. Brian was due home soon from the mission school. Perhaps, Edith suggested, we should take a break and return to Cafetal. Jim and I thought so too.

"Besides," Jim said, "we ought to have a letter from Tom on the next boat from Matto Grosso with news of his progress. Once he's back and we've got that paper in our hands, restraining the river-men from molesting the Indians, I'll feel a whole lot easier."

Only Dave looked unhappy. His usually smiling face was serious. "Gee, I hate to break off contact, even for a week or two, when everything's going so well."

"But *is* everything really going as well as we think?" I asked. This proved a good question. We could cite the increasing number of friendly contacts, the free interchange between our wives and children and theirs, their acceptance of our gifts, the gifts they were now bringing us in return, the real progress we were making in learning words of their language, and therefore the improvements in our communicating with them.

"But there are still a lot of things I don't like," I said, shaking my head. "For one thing, since we've been back, the chief has never come out. Then, remember that ever since the rivermen were here the Nhambiguaras have taken to whispering among themselves. And how about the nights we thought they were sneaking around our camp?"

I paused, then went on: "Sometimes I wonder if we aren't putting too much faith in their surface friendliness and not paying enough attention to what's going on in their minds." I reminded my friends of the stories Don Juan and other Bolivians told of the Indians' genius for deceit. Then I remembered something else. "And how about when they felt our arms and legs?"

"They'd get precious little meat off your skinny bones," said Dave. He grinned, we all chuckled, and this broke the somber mood. Dave got up and stretched. "Tell you what," he said. "You all go back to Cafetal and stock up as planned. I'll stay here by myself while you're gone and keep up the contact."

We voiced our protests, but Dave wouldn't listen. "I don't mind 'baching' it," he said. "I've done it many times in the woods in Washington and Oregon. Anyway, I'll have the dogs for company and the Lord will look after me."

I felt uneasy about this arrangement. Should the Nhambiguaras turn mean, Dave, even with the dogs and his gun to scare them off (he was an experienced hunter and a dead shot), would be no match for them. They might be prompted to attack one man alone, where they wouldn't risk it with a group of us. For several days we tossed our ideas back and forth. But Dave's determination remained unshaken.

So, on a bright November morning—this was still 1951—we loaded the dugout; when the mail boat returned from upriver we hitched on and said good-by to Dave. Helen and Edith were close to tears.

"This has been one of the happiest times of my life," Edith said. "Even though it's been hard, we've been blessed with fellowship. And for the first time I feel I've been actively fulfilled in the work to which we've dedicated ourselves."

As the cliff of Paredon slipped out of sight behind us, our hearts were happy for the progress and for having a part in this ministry. Our reservations about leaving Dave had for the moment been overcome. We had no inkling of the dark days ahead.

10

Dunkirk of the Soul

"I wonder what he's doing now?" Edith said. "I certainly hope the Indians won't cross the river and come up to camp while we're away."

The four of us were watching the jungle go by, the women in their hammocks with the children, Jim and I seated on the cargo. Our thoughts were again of Dave.

"Remember, they don't have any dugouts," I said lightly, trying to reassure her. But the thought of the shallow place upstream where they could wade across in this dry season made me uneasy.

"I can't help thinking I should have stayed with him," Jim said. He was frowning.

But from the moment, two days later, when our mail boat pulled into Cafetal in the late afternoon, we had no time to worry. Some neighbors, who had not seen us in several months, were waiting on the bank. They couldn't wait to hear about our adventure. They pelted us with questions: Had we really seen the Nhambiguaras up close? Had they shot arrows at us? Was it true they were cannibals? We answered them as best we could, as they accompanied us up to the house.

130

When we reached home, we saw that we had our hands full. Before we could even enter, I had to break up the big mud cell the hornets built around the padlock. Inside, the house had the typical damp, moldy smell of being shut up. With a housewife's zeal, Edith went about opening shutters and setting things in order.

The slanting light streaming in revealed havoc. The floor was littered with fragments of palm leaves fallen from the roof. Every corner was gray with cobwebs. And the mold!—mold on our shoes, mold on our clothes, mold on our books (which had also been chewed around the edges by hungry cockroaches). This was before we had learned to protect our volumes by spraying plastic coating on the bindings.

In a short time a home atmosphere was being restored. To keep the dust down, Edith sprinkled the dirt floor before sweeping. Connie found her "junk" box and got out her playthings. I split some wood and started a fire in the adobe brick oven. Since all our energies were needed to get the house straight, Edith prepared us the simplest possible supper—just pancakes. But how good they tasted!

A hot wind blowing out of the north forewarned us of a big storm within a few hours. In the evening our house was filled with visitors. Our stories about the Nhambiguaras had to be told and retold as different ones came in, until the roll of thunder sent our guests scurrying for home.

It was not until I had been in bed some time that my mind went back to Dave Yarwood. I could picture him lying in his bunk, with the lantern on the packing case beside him, reading his Bible. His dog "Sacky" would be dozing on the ground, now and then raising his head with one ear cocked at any strange sound.

All kinds of thoughts went through my mind: Dave Yarwood alone . . . tricky Indians, friendly Indians . . . no chief . . . meddlesome rivermen . . . forces of darkness . . . the power of God . . . the meaning of human decisions . . . Even the rhythmic pounding of the downpour could not lull me to sleep.

To quiet myself, I tried to concentrate optimistically on the bright picture of the work that lay ahead if all went well. I could see our having friendlier contacts with the Nhambiguaras, making progress with the language, eventually teaching them to read and write, finally being able to reach them with the simple Gospel message and with translations into their tongue of portions of the Scripture. And sometime—the final fulfillment—a healthy, growing, indigenous church of believers. It had happened elsewhere: why not here?

Then more troubled thoughts invaded this glowing dream. Beneath their friendliness what were the Indians really thinking? No chief . . . the problem of the nationals still unsettled . . . that inexplicable, brooding atmosphere of depression we so often felt when we were in their presence. . . . And Dave Yarwood there to face this alone.

The night air moved the big mosquito net over our bed. The storm had passed, but the air was still muggy. Beside me, Edith stirred in her sleep. I could hear the fish splashing in the river as clearly as if they were in the room.

I continued to think of Dave. Many of the fellows were close to me, but Dave was closest of all. I recalled some of the things he had done for me: such as the time on the trail when my knee went bad. "Here, boy, let me have that," he had said, and had added my heavy pack to his own. "I wouldn't be doing this job for all the money in the world," he used to say to me. "I'm doing it to show my appreciation to the Lord because he's done so much for me."

I remembered the time Dave had put his arm around one of the naked Nhambiguaras and told him in English of God's love for the Indians, and of how He had sent His Son to shed His blood for their redemption. The Indian put his lips to Dave's ear after each sentence or two and whispered back, in almost perfect English, everything Dave would be telling him. The Nhambiguaras were great mimics. The Indian's eyes sparkled with mischief. He thought it was some kind of huge joke. He didn't understand a word, and of course, Dave knew it. Not that it mattered to him—

he just had to unburden his soul. And perhaps it lifted up his hopes for the time when he would be able to tell that same story in the Nhambiguaras' own tongue, and the Indians would listen—and begin to understand.

Toward dawn, I drifted off into a restless slumber.

As the days passed, we waited anxiously. The mail boat bringing Brian had not come; and there was no word from Tom as to whether he had accomplished anything with the authorities in Matto Grosso.

"When Brian come, Mommy?" Connie would ask every few minutes.

"Any day now," Edith would reply with remarkable patience. Then Connie would go to explain this to her doll, who seemed the only one with time to listen to her constant chatter.

Since Brian liked to imitate everything I did, I busied myself making him a miniature wheelbarrow which would be ready for him when he came home. Then he could carry firewood in it, as I did in mine.

It was a great day when Bob Williams finally arrived on the mail boat, bringing Brian for his vacation. (The river was low, and the boat had run into trouble with sandbars.) Supper was a time of talk about school and the teachers, hikes, and parties. When the children were in bed we went over to the Ostewigs for a late evening snack and to bring Bob up to date. He was delighted and astonished to hear we had been able to become friends with the Nhambiguaras, after the first narrow escape on our surprise visit to their village.

"And what about the ones that were hanging around the day you and Jim went into the clearing?" Bob wanted to know. "Did any of them recognize you?"

"As near as I could tell from their sign language, two or three of them did," I replied. "But if so, they didn't seem to harbor any hard feelings."

The boat that had brought Brian and Bob was going only as far up the Guaporé as Rio Cabixi this trip. Then it was due back at Cafetal in four or five days. Since Rio Cabixi was about two-thirds of the way to Paredon and the closest settlement to our camp, we thought there was a good chance the boat might bring us some tidings of Dave. We also hoped that lack of news from Tom here in Cafetal meant he had perhaps gone straight back to join Dave at Paredon. We waited anxiously for its return.

It was almost dusk. The captain was just coming off the gangplank as Jim, Bob, and I ran up to meet the boat from Rio Cabixi. He had become a good friend. A slight, dapper man, full of Latin charm, he was quick with a ready smile that showed his flashing teeth, always with a gay quip or a joke of some kind on his lips.

This time his face was unsmiling. His manner was stiff, almost formal. He greeted us with the barest nod. "Come with me," he said. "I have something to tell you."

I saw he had no letter in his hand. Immediately I had a premonition of bad news. We followed him up the earthen steps.

At the top of the bank he stopped and faced us. The mosquitoes had come out of the jungle and were buzzing away overhead. In the fading light his face looked drawn. His dark eyes stared directly into mine. "Dave . . . your friend . . ." his voice quavered.

"Yes?"

"He is dead."

"Oh, no!"

He nodded.

I felt as though I had been struck hard in the pit of the stomach. Jim gasped. For a few seconds none of us was able to speak.

Then Jim said, "Are you sure? It's not one of those rumors?" The captain shook his head. "I am certain. It is no rumor."

"How did it happen?" Bob asked.

"I do not know much," said the captain. "But what I do know, I know for myself." He paused and looked out at the river as though trying to gather strength for what he had to tell us. "We were getting ready to leave Rio Cabixi to come down here, when three men arrived from upriver in a high state of agitation. They were tax collectors. They had planned to stay at your camp at

Paredon overnight, because, as you can imagine, tax collectors are not exactly welcome in the rubber settlements. But when they got there, no one was around. The camp was deserted.

"In the morning, they saw vultures circling in the sky above the other bank of the river. The men jumped in their dugout and went to have a look. On the sand by the high bank they saw the body of a man—a big man—a foreigner."

"That's Dave, all right," said Jim, his voice breaking.

"Did they—did they stop to bury him?" asked Bob.

"No," the captain said quickly. "They were too scared the same thing might happen to them. They cleared out as fast as they could and came right down to Rio Cabixi where I met them."

Night had closed in. With our flashlights making bright stabs into the dark ahead of us, we started up to our houses. We faced the hard job of breaking the news to our wives. The captain excused himself, saying he had to go. We thanked him for his kindness.

"I am sorry, very, very sorry," he said. Then he shook our hands and walked away. Bob said good-by to us and followed after him. He was leaving for Guajara Mirim on the same boat.

A lump swelled my throat until it ached. A sense of loss and desolation enveloped me. Jim and I went in and told Helen and Edith. They wept brokenheartedly. It was a long time before we found consolation in reminding ourselves that Dave had been promoted to the presence of the Lord, where he was finding his reward in eternal peace and joy.

After we had bowed our heads in prayer, Jim said, "We've got to go there and bury him. We'd better get our stuff together tonight so we'll be able to leave first thing in the morning." Our wives' faces showed their concern, but they were with us in our resolve.

Jim went to get some gas. I gathered together the necessary tools. No one had much sleep that night.

After an early start, Jim, a neighbor, and I traveled all day and continued on after nightfall. There was a moon to give us a little light. The air was damp and cool. I curled up on the crosspiece and tried to get some sleep. Shortly after I had dozed off, I was awakened by a sudden jolt that threw me to the bottom of the boat. A sharp pain stabbed my back. The Bolivian had fallen asleep and the dugout had rammed into the bank.

Toward late afternoon the next day we saw the handful of palm-thatched houses that was Rio Cabixi. My heart was so full of grief I hardly cared.

The rubber workers asked us to have supper. We wanted to push on, but there was no refusing them.

After the meal, we sat around talking in one of their houses. When we told them of our mission, they tried at first to prevent our going.

"So?" said one of them with a shrug. "Your friend is dead. You cannot bring him back to life. You will be killed, too. That's all you will accomplish." He gave a wave of his dirty, copper-colored hand, the indelible brand of one who works over smoking crude rubber. Several burst out into voluble Portuguese.

We tried to explain we could never rest until Dave had a proper Christian burial, and also that we had to stop at Paredon to bring back his personal possessions. But we could see this made no sense to them. They probably thought we were crazy.

"You got guns?" one older man asked.

"We always carry two or three for hunting," Jim said.

Silence.

"If they attack, you shoot?" asked another.

"No," I said with conviction, "I would not. We do not believe in killing."

"The Bible says, 'Thou shalt not kill,' " said Jim.

"But they kill your friend," argued the first one. "Don't you want to be revenged?" He slapped his brimless hat across his knee restlessly. (Hat brims catch the jungle thorns.)

"When I was a boy," I said, "all anybody had to do was to call me a name and the fight was on. Since then I've learned better. I can honestly say I have no feeling of revenge in my heart for those Indians—even though they did kill Dave. That has not changed my desire to reach them with the Gospel."

"So!" said one tall man, leaning forward. "You mean they send arrows at you and you only stand there and be dead, you do not shoot back?"

They exchanged wondering glances among themselves as if to say, "These men are clearly idiots and we do not understand them. But they are all right, they are on our side, so we must do what we can to protect them."

The tall man muttered something in Portuguese and pulled on his boots, the typical calf-length ones, with the trousers bulging from their tops. The rubber workers got up and went out. In a few minutes they were back with their guns.

"Look, we appreciate your help," Jim said, "but we wouldn't want you to shoot the Nhambiguaras either."

The tall man bared his teeth in a sardonic grin. "Don't worry—we won't shoot."

We didn't believe it. But to question the word of these cocky men might mean starting a fight, so we let it go. We made ready to leave together immediately.

The rubber hunters got out a flat-bottomed barge with a wooden roof and lashed it to the side of our dugout. We started on our sad journey. The sun had already sunk in the west, leaving only a glowing ember in the sky. Fog settled around us. We stretched out on boards and tried to make ourselves comfortable. The damp cold was penetrating. My back was hurting from the accident and kept me awake. I lay there listening to the drone of the outboard motor.

When we passed the sandbar where we had laid out our first gifts, it was near morning; the night was just beginning to gray. Farther on, we came to the spot where we had made our first real contact. Each place along the river brought special memories. At times, I could almost hear Dave's hearty laugh ring out. My heart ached.

About an hour after dawn, we went ashore at Paredon. A slight rain must have fallen during the night, for the ground was soft.

How desolate was the familiar scene. So often before, we had been greeted there upon landing by the sound of someone chopping wood, someone singing, a dog barking, the laughter of a child, the cheerful sounds of civilization—the beachhead of our fellowship in the vast unfriendly jungle.

Now all was hushed.

The Brazilians must have felt it, too, for they spoke no word and walked softly. Dawning sunlight, filtering through the branches, made strange shapes around us and gave the place an unearthly look.

Sadly, I started up the hill to our camp, then I stopped. On the step before me was a freshly broken palm leaf. My eyes fell on a fresh footprint—one made by a bare foot, not by a shoe. Nearby was another, then another, many others.

"They've been here!" exclaimed the tall Brazilian.

"That's what they do after they kill," said another. "I've heard it. They come in the night, steal the dead one's possessions, and burn his house down."

"We must have come in the nick of time," Jim said. "Maybe they heard our outboard and ran away."

"Maybe they're hiding in the woods right now," added the tall Brazilian.

The men from Rio Cabixi cocked their guns and held them at the ready. Cautiously scanning the leaves on either side, we climbed on.

Even sadder was the silence that brooded over the log cabin where, as Edith said, we had spent some of the happiest days of our lives.

My eyes blurred with tears as I went around, gathering up the homely everyday possessions that spoke so eloquently of Dave: his knapsack with the twisted strap so familiar to me; his well-thumbed Bible with the torn binding; his diary, open at the page where he had made his last entry; his lantern that he always read by. When I saw his jacket hanging from a peg, holding almost the shape of his husky frame, I had to turn away.

The chickens clucked feebly from the yard. I went out to see how they were, and came across "Sacky" lying on the ground on the edge of the clearing. He was so weak he could only look up at me with pitiful eyes, and thump his tail in greeting. The other dog, lying not far away, was in such bad shape I had to take him out in the woods and shoot him. I got a can of meat from the supplies and a pan of water for Dave's dog. He stirred and rose on unsteady legs. All the while, the rubber workers stood guard, alert, watchful for any movement in the jungle walls.

We took Dave's things and everything Tom had left behind and carried them down to the canoe. It was too dangerous to risk coming back for them. Then we paddled across the river.

It did not take us long to find the place the captain had described. I saw the black and white of the turkey feathers first . . . then the shafts of two arrows . . . then all that remained of Dave —not far from the water's edge, I saw his body. I tried to gain strength by reminding myself that this was only the poor house of clay, wherein had dwelt the soul of our brother in Christ—the soul that was now resting in eternal peace. But it was hard, so hard. Jim and I brought shovels from the canoe and began to dig a grave as deep as we could in the shady clearing.

While we struck away at the sand, the gnats, attracted by our sweat, swarmed down on us. The Brazilians, guns in hand, spread out, ready to shoot at any movement of a leaf. They were really jumpy now. We were thankful for their protection, which gave us at least some feeling of security. But our hearts were troubled, too, lest an Indian appear and they shoot him down, only to be shot by arrows in return. Our care of our comrade would have then led to another round of bloody warfare.

Jim and I finished the grave and laid poor Dave to his final rest. The worst part was pulling out the arrows—the two in his back which I had seen sticking up, two more from his chest. We fashioned a rude cross out of branches cut from a nearby tree. In a choking voice, I gave a few words of heartfelt prayer. Even the rough rubber workers felt the solemnity of the moment. They removed their brimless hats and stood with bowed heads—although their eyes remained watchful.

When the prayer was ended, we hurried for the dugout and started the outboard.

Until this moment, I had been unable to think about anything but the situation at hand. Now, for the first time, as we chugged down the peaceful river, with the danger receding behind us, dark misgivings pressed in on me with all the ominousness of an approaching storm. Had we done wrong in leaving Dave? Would this awful scene we had just been through have taken place had we stayed? Or would Jim and I and our families and Tom, too, all be lying there by Dave's side? How can one ever know at a given moment if his decision is the right one? How can one know what is the Lord's will? I would have a lot of soul-searching to do, a lot of accounting to my conscience, before peace could come again.

I can only reconstruct the events that led up to Dave's death. But through access to his diary, my talks with the tax collectors, and my intimate knowledge of the way he lived and thought, I can do so with reasonable accuracy.

I will begin with an entry from his diary (I am reproducing this from memory):

Today is December 2, a nice day. I was working around the place this morning when I heard somebody holler up from the river in Portuguese, "Anybody up there?"

"Yeah," I yelled back. "Come on up."

Along came three Brazilians. All slight and sallow. They looked more like clerks than rough-and-ready rivermen. One of them said, "We're from Matto Grosso. We're tax collectors. We're going along the river trying to collect taxes from the rubber workers."

I laughed.

"Guess they don't exactly roll out the welcome mat for you in the rubber settlements."

They laughed, too.

"No," one of them said. "We don't let them know we're coming. Otherwise they'd hide as much of their rubber as possible from us."

I fixed them a cup of coffee. I'm glad I know now how to make it the way they like it—brewed to the right potency and thickness.

We sat drinking our coffee. It was good to have people around for a change. Then I heard that long, low whistle coming from across the river. I put my cup down, went outside, and whistled back. I got an answering whistle. The tax collectors were sure curious. They wanted to know what was going on.

"Indians," I said. "That's their signal they want me to come across the river and meet them."

The Brazilians' eyes popped. They'd been traveling up and down the Guaporé for years and they'd never seen one. They begged me to take them along. I gave them a good talking-to first and they promised they'd behave themselves. They seemed like quiet, mild-mannered men and I thought they would, so I let them get into the dugout.

Seven Nhambiguaras were out on the sandbar waiting for us. Five of them were ones I recognized from former contacts. But two of them were new. They acted sort of surly but I didn't think anything of this. The new ones often did. We talked for awhile in sign language and traded gifts. The tax collectors were excited. Now they'd have something they could talk about when they went back to Matto Grosso. Pretty soon one of the Brazilians said to me, "Hey—that hard guy over there—is he the chief?"

I told him I didn't know because we'd never seen the chief. Then I started paying attention. This one was sure giving orders as if he *was* the chief. This was big stuff—for the first time, maybe, I was really seeing Number One. I tried to make signs to the others, asking if this was the headman. If they knew what I was saying, they didn't let on.

But this chief—if he was one—didn't get any more friendly. I thought we'd better pull out of there and we did.

Soon after we got to camp, my visitors went off, saying they might be back in a day or two. In the afternoon I heard the whistle again. This time one of the new men—not the chief, the other one—wanted to trade his bow and arrow for a machete. I paddled over to camp and got one.

I'm sure glad that everything is going so well. I hope the Ostewigs and the Porterfields come back soon. We have only a month or so in which to work before the rainy season begins. Then the lowlands on the Brazilian side by the river will be flooded and it will be hard to make contact.

Another entry:

December 4. This was a beautiful day. It was nice and cool in the morning. The birds were singing and that old woodpecker was trying to knock his brains out against a tree. I enjoyed reading my Bible and talking to the Lord. He seems very close.

Oh, what a life! It's so peaceful and uncomplicated out here beyond civilization. No noise, no smells from motors; no whistles, bells, or alarm clocks to keep reminding you how fast time is flying. No rush, no harsh words. No bills, no rent to think about. No upsetting news from the outside world.

Nine tribesmen came out today. I made real progress. Picked up quite a few more words. The two new ones were there again, including the one who speaks with authority. That one: is he really the chief? I would give anything to know. I asked questions in sign language. But I did not get any answer I could understand. There were also two more new ones. The new ones, including the one who may be the chief, hung back. They did not join in the contact. I thought they were asking: Where are the Brazilians? But I couldn't be sure. On the whole, though, the atmosphere was friendly. We'll see what happens tomorrow . . .

That was the last entry in Dave's diary. What happened after that I can only piece together, for there were no witnesses until the tax collectors discovered his body. In the cabin at Paredon we found a half-opened can of Spam and a pan of rice on the wood stove. Dave, then, must have been getting ready to eat his noonday dinner when he heard the signal to cross the river.

There he must have walked into an ambush. One arrow was fancier than the others, with more decorations, more feathers; it could have belonged to the chief. That, plus one other, was embedded in his chest. Two more arrows were in his back. Dave must have been shot from ambush, therefore, as he crossed the shady clearing. Then, as he turned to run back to his canoe, he must have been shot again.

Why? Did the chief think he was one of the nationals, or that he was working with the nationals? Was the chief determined to get his revenge on them for (as he thought) trying to kidnap their wives? Or was such a fate planned for all of us right along? Had their friendship been merely a pretense to get all the gifts they could out of us before finishing us off? These questions—questions to which there were no answers—tormented me for weeks.

When news of Dave's death reached the States, the reaction, as one might expect, was mixed. Some thought it but one more example of foolhardy missionaries who ran needless risks. Many others felt a prick of conscience that in their lives of comfort they had paid so little attention to those who were carrying forward the work of evangelizing the lost in the front lines. In time, it became clear to to the world that Dave, by his death, had won his everlasting place on the heroic roll of Christian martyrs. Some were stirred to dedicate themselves to taking up the work of the fallen soldier.

There began for me the darkest time of my life, a time when I was shaken to the very depths of my being. The whole purpose of my life—my faith itself—was about to crumble into nothingness.

I dreaded to see darkness come, for my nights were filled with horror. I had nightmares—not just now and then but one after the other—every time I closed my eyes. Nightmares which were more real than reality itself, from which I awoke shouting and screaming, nightmares in which I stood unable to move, feeling the physical pain of arrows in my chest, assailed me.

The days were not much better. Edith, the children, and I were alone. A week after we had learned of Dave's death, Jim and Helen returned to Cochabamba to take up the teaching of Spanish. Through every waking moment I was in a state of perpetual torment, assailed by doubts and self-accusations. I suppose doctors would have said I was having a nervous breakdown; but there were no doctors within miles to tell me so.

What made it all the worse was that my inner anguish cut me off so completely from my family. They would look at me with sad, troubled eyes, trying to understand the emotional storm tearing me apart. Edith did her best to tempt my appetite with unusually tasty meals. But I could not eat. I grew gaunt and haggard. I gave up trying to drink coffee when anyone else was present, because my hand shook so in getting the cup to my mouth I feared people would talk and ask me questions. My back hurt from the old injury and I could not work. Brian and even Connie brought water from the river in their tin kettles and took to trundling in wood in Brian's wheelbarrow.

And outwardly, life could have been so pleasant. I had time now to take Brian fishing. But when he caught a twenty-pound catfish,

I could not share his glee. It was something happening far off, outside of me. I was consumed with my own churning emotions.

One incident brought me to realize, with a jolt, the depths of uselessness into which I had fallen. The night before, a jaguar had raided our chicken coop and made off with one of the chickens. Brian took one look at his mother's face as she told about this and said confidently, "Don't worry, Mom. I'll protect you."

That pulled me up short, but the inner turmoil soon possessed me once more. I knew that I was cranky. Sometimes I would speak sharply to my loved ones in answer to a question. Then I would ask their forgiveness to ease my conscience.

Off beyond the edge of Cafetal was an ox trail through the jungle. I could find peace there, and solitude—except for the mosquitoes. I went out there and paced up and down day after day, all by myself, searching my soul for answers.

Someone had warned me once never to try to come to a decision about anything when either ill or afflicted. In my mind I knew the wisdom of that warning. But I could not follow it. Deep down within every man are his convictions, the pillars of his character and his integrity, which help support him in times of stress. I groped for these within myself, only to find them weak and shaky, about to be swept away, leaving me aimless for the rest of my life.

No one but I will ever know how close I came to defeat. It was so easy to give up. The powers of darkness closed in. A small, nagging voice kept whispering to me, "Somewhere in the States is a nice country church that needs a pastor. There you would find no struggles, no hardships, no setbacks, no disappointments."

"But," my conscience would protest, "to back down now would be 'chicken.'"

"Who would ever know?" the other voice whispered beguilingly. "You can just say you're returning because your health is bad. That's true enough, isn't it?"

Yes, it was true enough. But I also knew that if I could win my spiritual battle, my physical health would improve fast enough right in Cafetal. The voice came again, pressing its advantage:

"And what have you got to show for all those experiences that are giving you nightmares? For all those labors, hardships, sufferings—even death—that you say are the lot of the pioneer missionary? If you go on and try once more, what will happen then? More of the same: no tribes reached, no souls saved—death the only ending. And whose death next? Another of your comrades? Maybe your own? What's the point of it all? And how do you know your decisions have been so right?"

That touched the sorest spot. Had I been wrong in allowing the nationals to go with us on contact to the Nhambiguaras? Had I been wrong in returning to base at Cafetal, leaving Dave to go to his death alone?

For perhaps the thousandth time, my mind went over the chain of events leading up to the tragedy. I remembered the night we had reached the decision to let Dave stay on at Paredon. I remembered how we had prayed for guidance. I remembered the peace that had come afterward. That was the peace I sought now.

Had I made a mistake? Was a mistake possible in the light of God's overall plan? On the other hand, to excuse one's own actions by saying always that one is led by the Lord could lead to careless and irresponsible living. I knew that God's grace does not grant liberty to sin. If I had made a mistake, I wanted to face it, so I would not make it again.

My thoughts went round and round . . . I was unable to concentrate on reading. I was too confused to pray.

As we go through life, how little are we aware that the seed of simple, homely truths, implanted in the heart by others, may burst into flower just when they are needed. On one of my lonely vigils on the ox trail in the jungle such a truth came to me. It had been implanted in my heart so long before that I cannot remember whether it was something I had read or something I had heard in a forgotten sermon. In the darkest hour of my despair, when I knew I was on the verge of cracking up, it came to me.

It was simply this: A city policeman, holding up his hand to stop traffic, is, after all, only a man like other men. Then why does every motorist, every truck driver, obey his gesture, his whistle? Because the policeman is the representative of authority, the authority of the state, of society, which every individual must respect. So every Christian is representative of the authority of God. In every one of us is vested God's omnipotence. We have but to be aware of it and to use it against the traffic of darkness. As the Scriptures advise, I resisted Satan in the name of Jesus Christ.

I felt strengthened immediately. I called upon the Lord to rout the dark thoughts, the haunting memories that were afflicting me. I returned to my family with a smile on my face. That night, for the first time in weeks, I slept. The hounding thoughts, suggestions, and self-condemnations began to lose their persuasiveness. Then they came no more.

Now that I could read Scripture purposefully again, I found comfort in the verse from I Corinthians 10:13: "There hath no temptation taken you but such as is common to man: but God is faithful, who will not suffer you to be tempted above that ye are able; but will with the temptation also make a way to escape, that ye may be able to bear it."

I put from my heart all thoughts of giving up the battle and returning to the States. At last I could think clearly about plans for the future.

But since further contact with the Nhambiguaras was entirely out of the question, at least for the immediate future, and since I still had doubts about the wisdom of my own judgment, what could I do?

That, too, was soon to be revealed to me. But putting my hard-won experience at the service of others, I would see to it that Dave's death had not been for nothing. Surely that was the essence of the Christian teaching.

At that time I had no idea how or where the opportunity would come. But come it would, I knew.

Once more my heart was at peace.

11

Grip of the Swamp

Two months had passed since Dave's death. Now that I had emerged from the "dark night of my soul," I realized life had to go on. The real problems of the present and future kept challenging me and pulling me out of my inactivity. It was time to go back downriver to Guajara Mirim, then on to Cochabamba to take Brian to school. While there Edith and I would attend a field conference. The trip would give us the opportunity to seek a new place in which to serve.

Everything was packed and ready. Edith, Brian, Connie, and I waited nervously for the mail boat. There was no telling when it would come—or in what weather. We were happy when it showed up on a clear afternoon.

About five o'clock we cast off. Heavy, dark clouds were beginning to appear. Night came on fast—an inky-black night. As I zipped Brian and Connie into their mosquito nets, I hoped I wasn't zipping them into a trap should the boat sink. Edith and I lay wide awake in our hammocks. Surely, I told myself, it couldn't happen again. Yet every noise, every squeak, aroused my anxiety. I wanted it to be an easy trip, for Edith was in her third month's

147

pregnancy, a difficult time. At least the river was high, which was good, because it lessened the chances of hitting a rock or a sandbar. Sleepless hour followed sleepless hour, until at last we dozed.

A jolt awakened me.

"Here we go again!" I said to myself. I shot out of my hammock, and ran to get the children out of theirs. Glancing at the stern, I saw in the dim light of the lantern that the gunwale was still a few inches above water. I let the children sleep on for the moment. The sudden jolt had also awakened Edith, and she struggled out of her hammock.

Water was oozing through the floor boards, and a crewman worked feverishly to stuff rags into cracks.

"What happened?" I asked.

"Hit some submerged grassland," he muttered over his shoulder as he worked. "Threw the bow up in the air. We're okay—just so the stern doesn't go under."

Now others joined him. They were alternately bailing water and stuffing up the cracks. I went to the side and looked out. Four men, standing chest deep in the water, shoved with their hands, while three others on board pushed with poles. The boat shifted slightly; there was a scraping sound; the stern rose. We were free! Under their mosquito nets, Brian and Connie still slept, as if in a gently rocking cradle. But Edith and I were wider awake than ever, awaiting the dawn.

By the morning light we saw the crewmen still plugging new leaks. No doubt they would have to continue doing so for the rest of the trip. That was disturbing, for we had almost five hundred miles yet to go. At our present speed of about five miles an hour, it would take us another five days and five nights. What bothered me most of all was the chance we might spring a big leak during the night and ship enough water to sink the boat before it was discovered. We dispensed with the mosquito nets.

Day followed night with only minor crises. Weariness crept up on us. It was difficult to sleep: we had no protection against the mosquitoes' nightly onslaught; the hammocks vibrated with the banging motor; and we were on edge, half-expecting another crash.

But all went well. Only a day and a night remained before we would reach Guajara Mirim. Edith and I relaxed. During the early afternoon I passed the time playing "Can you guess what I'm thinking?" with Brian. When he tired of that, his mother took him over, and I went to join some of the other passengers at the railing. They were all quiet and looking anxiously at the sky, where clouds were gathering along the horizon. Gradually, as they stretched across the west, our world was reduced to darkness.

"Looks like we're in for a real one," a man beside me said. The light wind, already grown stronger, was beginning to kick up waves. I helped the crew nail down the canvas tarpaulin on the windward side to keep the waves from sloshing into the boat. The diesel banged away; the boat hugged the shore.

The whole atmosphere was tense with electricity, awaiting the first lightning bolts to relieve the pent-up charge. The clouds rose higher; the storm drew near. Flashes appeared among the billowing clouds. The wind whipped the waves higher and higher.

I glanced uneasily at the captain. He was standing by the rail with a couple of traders. The crew were working feverishly, for new leaks had appeared fore and aft. Waves were breaking over the combing; two passengers joined the crew in bailing.

The captain shouted something in Portuguese to the pilot. The boat changed course. I happened to look toward shore. To my amazement, I noticed it had receded by several hundred yards. The captain lurched by me and I caught a whiff of alcohol. Now I could see that we were headed for the middle of the river (which was about a mile wide at this point) where the waters were extremely rough. The captain, who was apparently drunk, had given the order to cross the river at the worst possible moment. Rain was pelting down hard; the storm had closed in. I looked again at the captain. He was stumbling aimlessly about over the cargo, bawling unintelligible orders to everyone in sight.

I was concerned about Edith. She was sitting with Brian, Connie, and me, huddled under the canvas. The children, sensing the danger, wanted to be in our arms. Suddenly a terrible crash rocked the boat—then another. A third one really shook us. Other women passengers cried out with fright. The mail boat and the diesel boat had loosened their hawsers just enough so that in the rough water they were banging away as though attacking each other. I clung to a post and tried to make out where we were, but in the blinding rain I could see neither shore. The crew, bailing violently, barely held their own against the waves pouring over the side. I thought we would sink for sure.

I heard shouting and saw a passenger arguing with the captain and screaming his protests against crossing the river in such waves. The captain was waving his arms like a madman. It looked as though the fight would start any second. I maneuvered toward them. But two other passengers got there first, and separated them.

All any of us could do now was bail, and bail we did. Two crewmen ran by me, tearing up rags as they went. Apparently a new and larger leak had been discovered.

Someone gave a shout. The misty line of the far shore was coming into view. The banging of the boats let up, as the pilot swung their bows around into the waves. The wind and the rain abated somewhat.

In another ten minutes we had reached the riverbank. The captain, sobered by what had happened, gave orders to tie up until the storm had passed. The passengers, who had been badly shaken, calmed down. Few words were spoken; we were all glad to be alive. About an hour later, with the waves subsiding, our journey was resumed.

The following day we made port at Guajara Mirim. As we hiked along the path to the Sharps' home, we heard once more the asthmatic wheeze of the wood-burning engine. It was music to our ears. Passing the station, we saw people climbing aboard the cars for the two-day, two-hundred-mile trip downriver to Porto Velho. How we wished at that moment there were a railroad to Cafetal!

That evening we sat around in the cool twilight on the veranda of the Sharps' house. It seemed a lifetime since we had been there last—on that memorable evening before we left for Cafetal. So much had happened since then. My whole life had been turned upside down. I had been tested as never before.

A new missionary family were staying with Lyle and Lila Sharp. They were Wilbur and Dorothy Abbey, their two grade-school-age daughters, and a three-year-old boy. The Abbeys had just arrived from a small town in northern California, where Wilbur was a mail carrier. Wilbur reminded me of myself as I had been when Edith and I first went to Guajara Mirim. Filled with determination and missionary zeal, he could hardly wait to reach some tribe.

We talked for awhile of missionary work and of what was going on back home. As the evening wore on and the others went to bed, Lyle and I remained for a heart-to-heart talk.

For the first time I was able to pour out my whole story. What comfort, what solace it was, to be able to unburden myself to Lyle. He was familiar with what had happened to Dave. But only now was I able to tell him of the depths of my inner struggle—something I had been unable to communicate by letter. I also told him of my rededication, and of how I was about to begin my quest for a way to serve others.

Lyle listened intently. His deep-set eyes were warm with sympathy. Now and then he asked a question. Otherwise he let me talk. He seemed to understand completely what I had been through.

It was not until after I had talked about an hour and was beginning to run down that Lyle said quietly, "I may have just the opportunity you are looking for. How would like to help us reach the Macurapis?"

"The Macurapis? Who are they?" The name was strange to me.

Lyle smiled. "I'm not surprised," he said. "We never would have heard of them, either, if I hadn't happened to run into some traders in a store in Guajara Mirim who have had some dealings with them."

"Where are they?" I asked.

"Well, you know where the Rio Mequenes empties into the

Guaporé, about forty miles below Cafetal."

"Yes," I replied. "The mail boat stopped there when I was on it."

"All right. About sixty miles due east is where the Macurapis live. Sixty miles, that is, as the crow flies."

"In other words, meaning a hundred and a quarter or a hundred and fifty miles by trail or river."

"That's a fair guess, I should say."

"Doesn't sound too far," I said.

"Ah, but here's the catch," Lyle went on. "The area in between is one vast, dismal swamp. I've heard it extends for some three or four hundred miles along the Guaporé on the Brazilian side and is abouty thirty miles wide. I understand rubber workers cross it once in awhile—but nobody else." Now it was Lyle's turn to unburden himself. "I've been living here too long on station," he said, "in comparative comfort, helping supply other missionaries like you. I feel it's my turn to go into a tribe. And now that the Abbeys have arrived to help us, and another missionary family is coming to take my place here, this is my chance."

I had momentary doubts. Did Lyle really feel I was essential? Or was he presenting this opening because of what it would mean to me?

"But do you really need me?" I asked.

He laughed. "Look, Bruce. Let's face it. Wilbur and I are both a couple of green hands. We're in good shape physically, but neither of us has ever been on the trail. What we need above all is somebody with your experience in making contact and living out in the jungle."

His earnestness reassured me. I brought the conversation back to the Macurapis.

"What do you know about this tribe?"

"Not much."

"Are they savages?"

"I suppose the answer is yes—and no. They run around naked. They kill their game with bows and arrows. But they seem to get along pretty well with the neighboring rubber workers. Some Macurapis even work for them. Honestly, we don't expect them to give us much trouble. In fact, we plan to set up permanent camp on the other side of the swamp. From there we can make contact. We plan to take our families."

This gave me pause. I couldn't help thinking of the Nhambiguaras, how we had once put our trust in them, and what had happened as a result.

"Take it easy, Lyle," I said. "Better find out what you're getting into, first."

Lyle was silent. He stretched his legs, thrusting his hands in his pockets. "There's risk in all contacts," he said, looking out into the night. "We know that. The Lord will give us His protection. We know that too. At the same time it would be wrong to expose our families to unnecessary dangers." He turned to me. "That's why we need your advice and the benefit of your experience, as well as your help."

"Okay. I'm with you," I said, knowing that Edith would agree.

A great burden had been lifted from my heart.

During Edith's pregnancy, I did not want to go where I would be completely cut off from communication. It would therefore be some time before the expedition started. But there was a lot to be done by way of preparation; and now that I had a purpose in my life, I did not mind the waiting.

It was arranged that I would take the Sharp children and Brian to the opening of the February school term in Cochabamba. The Abbeys had already sent their two girls to school in Brazil. They planned to take their three-year-old boy with them. Meanwhile, the Sharps and the Abbeys would begin to buy and pack supplies and household goods. Then they would go upriver and build their forward base at the mouth of the Rio Mequenes.

One evening, about five months after our return to Cafetal, Lyle and Lila showed up. We were expecting them as we had exchanged letters during that time. They had written about the thatch-roofed house they were building and about the arrival of their provisions and possessions. Lila kindly offered to stay with Edith until after the baby was born.

Lyle had a lot to tell us. Wilbur and he, after several exploratory trips with a Brazilian guide, now had a better idea of what we would be up against. "It's some swamp, Bruce, that's all I can say. We were sure glad we had a guide to show us the way the first time."

I asked him if they'd had any bad experiences.

"Just a few brushes with some Yoperrohobobos, that's all. We met a party of alligator hunters. They had a couple of critters that measured at least twenty feet long, although we didn't see any others. They said there were a lot of anacondas in there—but we didn't see any of those, either, I'm happy to say."

"Did you learn any more about the Macurapis?"

"Only a little—from our guide. They seem peaceable enough. One did kill another Indian about a year ago. But they haven't bothered the nationals. We found out one thing: they speak only a few words of Portuguese. So we'll have to stay long enough to learn their language before we can bring them the Gospel."

At least this didn't sound as hopeless as reaching the Nhambiguaras. If we could just get across that swamp!

While Edith and Lila were doing the dishes, Lyle got out a map and some sketches and gave me a briefing. "There are no paths to follow. It's either water or grass—with muck underneath. In your boat, you strike out like so, steering by compass. When you reach about the middle of the swamp, at around this point"—he made an "X" on the map—"you see a certain clump of palm trees."

"Aren't there more than one clump of trees in there?" I asked. "If there are, we could get lost pretty easily."

Lyle shrugged and went on. "At the trees, you must change course, so. Then in about five hours—if you're still going in the right direction—you come to some relatively clear water, with lily pads floating on it." Lyle made another "X." "You keep going, and before long, if you haven't got off course, you see a hump in the trees in the distance that looks like this." He quickly sketched the hump, then went back to the map. "Heading for the hump, you eventually reach a small creek, here; and nearby, on this side, lives a family working the wild rubber."

"Clear as mud," I said, and added, "We'd better have a couple of compasses, in case one goes haywire. Ever hear about that missionary in the jungles of Mexico who had three compasses?"

He hadn't.

"Well, first off he had his regular pocket compass. But he thought *that* one might go haywire, so he brought a much bigger one along to check the small one. Then it occurred to him they could both go on the blink—this is true, mind you. So he packed in compass number three to check on the first two—a big ship's compass!"

Our joking and storytelling, however, soon gave way to the more serious business of making plans. Every detail of supply, transportation, and emergency measures was gone over with great care.

A few days went by. I will never forget the morning Edith's labor pains began. I looked out the window when I got up and was happy to see bright sunshine. Although most of the early morning haze had cleared, the sky was still a misty blue. From the window I could look down the row of huts, the smoke filtering up through their roofs as the neighbor women prepared breakfast. Then I heard Edith calling me.

I am sure most doctors would deplore the conditions we faced. I began to build up the fire to boil some water. A few days before we had already sterilized the bandages, pads, and instruments by wrapping them in pieces of newspaper, sticking them in the oven, then extracting them when the paper looked sufficiently scorched. And yet the room had, in its way, some slight resemblance to a hospital surgery room. Carefully, Lila and I laid out white sheets, syringe and needle, scissors, thread, gauze, antiseptic, and a baby basket. As the pains increased, I kept the water boiling and helped Lila with the last-minute scrubbing. It was not my first experience as a midwife—I had helped deliver the Ostewigs' first child two years before—but delivering my own child was something else again! Lila was a rock. Having grown up on a Midwestern farm, she was the embodiment of the competence and calm bred by that way of life. A delicate appearance belied her inner strength.

Edith was in an agony of labor for several hours; then the baby started to come. But after the child's head appeared, it stopped. The rest of the body would not move. The face was beginning to turn blue. It was hard for me not to panic. Lila discovered that the umbilical cord was wrapped tightly around the child's neck. She tried to loosen it, but was unable to. I took over. I couldn't budge it. I worked frantically at it, pulling, twisting. Finally, and probably in the nick of time, I did get it loose. Our little girl was safe and sound. With a good paddling, Gwendolyn began to breathe—in fact, for an hour or more afterward she yelled her protest against the rough handling she had received from her father.

I was now free to help move the Sharps and Abbeys to the tribe. A few weeks before, a couple named Ewart and Jean Sadler had arrived to replace the Ostewigs at Cafetal—Jim and Helen having decided to continue teaching Spanish in Cochabamba. Ewart, a tall, lanky Canadian, was a former radio technician. Anxious to reach the Indians, he offered to go with us; we eagerly accepted. So, with Edith and Gwendolyn and Connie in Jean's care, Lyle and Lila, their three-year-old boy John Allen, Ewart, and I departed in two boats for the outpost at Rio Mequenes, where Dorothy, Wilbur, and their boy were waiting.

Wilbur welcomed us happily. He said all their supplies were there now, about a ton-and-a-half of them, including household necessities. We began to pack them carefully in Lyle's short and wide aluminum boat, and in my twenty-eight-foot dugout canoe. Our trip had to be precisely timed: once we got in, then out, there would be no chance to make the trip with supplies again for the next ten months, since the swamp dries up enough to make it unnavigable for most of the year.

The packing took all day. Since there was no time to lose, the two families, Ewart, and I left early the next morning. Ewart and I handled the dugout, while the Abbeys and Sharps went in the other boat.

For the first hour we glided along the cool, dark waters of the Rio Mequenes. Shortly, Lyle's boat, which was in the lead, turned off into some lily pads and on into tall grass. Then I had my first sight of the swamp. I had never seen anything like it. Stretching from horizon to horizon, as far as the eye could reach, was one level, forlorn desolation, an empty wasteland of water and grass, then more water and more grass.

The slight breeze, which had brushed our faces while we were on the river and kept us refreshed, was gone now. I felt as though we had been plunged into a hot steamy shower room heavy with the mingled odors of decaying vegetation and dead fish. The sun beat down on us mercilessly; we were thankful for our straw hats.

Our boats slowed and came to a halt in a tough tangle. Grass was twisted around the propellers and had to be cut loose. In front of me I saw Lyle getting out his poles, and I followed suit. The rubber workers had taught us how to make the poles. Fifteen feet long, and with a crotch at one end, they were a necessity in swamp navigation. We jabbed them down through the grass, which rose two feet above the surface. At about seven feet down the crotch held. On the count of three, we would heave with all our strength and the boats would lurch ahead a few feet and stop again. Another count, another push. After half an hour of this, I was soaked with perspiration. We stopped to rest. The sweat fairly ran in streams from my chin and the end of my nose. I plopped down on some of the cargo beside Ewart, who had also been pushing hard. Both of us felt as though we had already done a day's work —and we had barely started.

We had struggled along in this way for four or five hours, when Lyle called out joyfully, "There's that clump of trees I've been watching for."

I was skeptical, and very tired. "I hope you're right. To me it looks like a lot of other clumps I've seen."

Lyle tried to explain to me how this clump was different. I remained skeptical. We changed direction. I searched the horizon for a landmark. But all I could see ahead was more of the same: the endless grass, and the mirrored, blinding glitter of the sun on the water in between. By midafternoon, our hands had many broken blisters, our muscles were quivering; but still we pushed at the count of three. The heat was taking a heavy toll of our energy. It was easy now to become slack. Cries of "Careful! You're rocking!" were more and more frequent. A cloud appeared. In a few minutes we were drenched with tropical rain. It was a welcome change from the scorching sun. We couldn't get any wetter than we already were from perspiration, so we went on poling through the downpour.

The rain stopped as suddenly as it began. We had our dinner right in the boats. The women opened some cans of pork and beans. For dessert we had "jungle pudding," a mixture of canned lemon juice and sweetened condensed milk which is self-thickening and tastes like lemon pie filling. The meal was topped off with a surprise: some oatmeal cookies our wives had baked before leaving Cafetal.

There was no possibility of getting to high ground by nightfall. We were caught right in the middle of the swamp and would have to sleep in the boats. We found a spot with relatively little grass and rearranged the boxes of cargo so as to stretch out on them. With clearer area around us, we had a better chance to spot any approaching snakes or alligators. Yet, weary as we were, we hardly dared fall asleep, for fear of falling off the cargo and into the water. Waiting for drowsiness to come, we cracked jokes back and forth.

The only sound was the croaking of frogs. I wondered if there were any alligators nearby. How often I had heard their grunts while camping along the riverbank! Just for fun, I thought I would try to imitate them. I let out an *"Ummmmmm bah! Ummmmmm bah-yah-yah!"*

Immediately, from all around us came an answering chorus:

"Ummmmmm bah! Ummmmmm bah-yah-yah!" There were at least a dozen or more! We must have camped right in the middle of an alligator colony. The women squealed.

"Now we're in for it," said Wilbur. "What if you gave their mating call?—or challenged them to a fight?"

We did not dare go to sleep where we were. We all fell to and rearranged our supplies so we wouldn't roll off. Gradually, as the *"Ummmmmm bah!"* chorus died away, we dozed fitfully.

The next day we resumed our painfully slow progress of poling through the swamp. Often we four men would get out and shove the boat along, while the women pushed with the poles. Once, Lila let out a cry. A deadly Yoperrohobobo was heading straight toward us. How we scrambled to get back into that boat! The confusion must have frightened the snake, for it took off in another direction. But it was some time before we could bring ourselves to get back into the water again—and then only when we had to.

Toward dusk we saw high land. Now we could cook and get a good night's sleep in our jungle hammocks. It was a great relief psychologically, too, because confinement to a few square yards can make a boat seem like a prison after awhile. We had quite forgotten the mosquitoes that would be waiting for us on shore in clouds, and we passed an uncomfortable night.

The next morning we found we could follow a small river, the Rio Colorado, that emptied into the swamp. We were overjoyed. But our elation didn't last long. The stream was choked with a tangle of lily pads and a kind of grass we hadn't seen before. We tried poking the twisted mass with our poles, but the ends went right on through.

"Let's try chopping it with our machetes," suggested Lyle.

That didn't work either, so we got out and trod down the chopped mass, alternately hacking and walking. This way we were able to make some progress.

While hanging on to the side of the boat and stomping down tangled masses of grass, I suddenly felt an irritating itch around my ankles. It spread up my legs. My first thought was that it must be ants crawling on me. But how could there be ants out here in the swamp? In an instant the stinging was all over me, from head to foot.

"Hey!" Wilbur yelled just then. "I feel like I'm on fire."

"So do I!" Lyle shouted. "But I don't see anything!"

"Man, it's terrible!" Wilbur cried. "What can it be?"

Up till this moment I had thought it was my skin that was affected. Now I knew it was my nerves. My whole body felt like one bundle of violin strings, drawn to the breaking point. The women sat watching us, sympathetic but puzzled. They were totally unable to understand what was happening. So were we, for that matter.

My brain was on fire. It was all I could do to keep from screaming. I could still think rationally, but I did not know for how long. If there is such a thing as an instant nervous breakdown, I was having it now. But what was causing it?

Then there came to my mind the stories I had heard of poisonous weeds with which the Indians were able to paralyze fish so they could scoop them up in their hands, of strange fungus growths that had a similar effect. Had the blades of our machetes released some such fluid that was attacking our nervous systems?

I shuddered to think of the women alone in the swamp with four men on their hands either helpless or on the verge of madness. Driven to a frenzy by the stinging, we crawled back into the canoes and, using our paddles, shoved on through the grass with all our strength. Finally, ahead, loomed a beautiful stretch of clear water. We jumped in. Slowly, the stinging subsided; the terrifying tightness of our nerves eased off. In a little while we were back to normal once more.

We all agreed we wouldn't try any more chopping.

By nightfall we reached another rubber camp on the Rio Colorado. The next day we came to the Rio Terebinto, which Lyle had marked on his map. In spite of its impressive name, it was no more than a deep creek about thirty feet wide. The going was easy at first. But before long we found the channel choked with jams of mahogany logs. Mahogany is a very hard wood, and we had to chop the key logs all the way through before they would give way and break the jam. We traveled on the Terebinto for several days, sometimes having to cut so many logs that we covered no more than five miles in a day. Every night we made a new camp.

The women's clothes were almost as badly torn as ours. Trees and vines often "clasped hands" over narrow spots in the river, blocking our passage. We would tell the women to put dishpans in front of their faces. Then we would open the motors wide and plow ahead as far as possible—sometimes making ten to twenty feet in one thrust. At times, thousands of ants would tumble down on us; or again, we would find ourselves right under a hornet's nest and unable to move. After one of these encounters, Lila had nineteen stings. We were worried about her, as she was about three months pregnant. All we could do was fight like mad to get past the tangle, and then "lick our wounds."

The animal life proved fascinating to the youngsters. Snakes, monkeys, and alligators were everywhere. One day, the Sharp boy spotted some large monkeys in the trees. Lyle made a move to cross the river. Then he veered away suddenly.

"What's the matter?" I called. He did not answer. Following the direction of his hypnotized stare, I saw what I took at first to be the trunk of a green-and-brown vine, twisted in the strangest convolutions. Looking a little higher, I saw, resting on top of it, a flat, triangular head, with a forked tongue darting in and out. Then I knew: a boa constrictor. Furthermore, it was a hungry one. I had been told that after a boa has eaten a deer or a wild pig, it will lie in a state of torpor for months while it digests its meal. But when it is coiled, that means it is poised ready to seize and crush any living creature that comes within range.

"Better get him!" I called in a hushed voice. "We don't want him hanging around when we go ashore."

Lyle raised his gun. A shot rang out. The green-and-brown folds thrashed, twitched, then hung straight down in two limp, parallel lengths. It was the biggest boa I had ever seen—it must have been about twenty feet long. Now I'd have something to tell Brian when I got back. He'd get a kick out of this.

Before dark we found a fine camping spot a little farther up-stream. We agreed not to unload the boats because we were so tired.

Once, during the night, I was awakened by a loud splash, but I paid no attention, thinking it was only the fish in the river. A little later I heard a clanking of gasoline tins; yet I couldn't be sure I hadn't dreamed it.

At the crack of dawn I peered out of my mosquito net. Lyle's boat was there, but the dugout was gone.

"Hey, Lyle! You awake?"

"Huh? What? What?"

He struggled up to a sitting position. I could see the top of the outboard just above the water.

"The canoe is sunk."

Lyle was out of his hammock in one bound. The others followed him.

"The provisions!" he moaned. "About a fourth of everything we have is in that canoe. And our supplies have got to last for ten months. Come on—let's see what we can salvage."

"Wait a minute," I cautioned. "I think I know what made those noises last night. It was an alligator. He must have got into the boat, going after those bananas. He may still be hanging around here."

"Can't help it," said Lyle. "We've got to save our food."

We four men jumped in and groped for the sacks and boxes. The sacks of rice weighed about a hundred and twenty pounds dry and at least twice that soaking wet. With much grunting and heaving we got it all out on the ground to dry. Lyle looked ruefully at the sacks of corn.

"We'll have to plant it the minute we get to our base," he said. "It'll start sprouting right away. Don't let me forget, now—everything depends on it."

The women gazed sadly at the dried peaches, on which they had counted as a delicacy to last many months.

"We'll have to eat those right away," Lila said. She put the kettle on to boil them. And so we did. Peaches in every guise were a featured item on our menu at every meal until we had eaten them all.

In three more days of hard travel, we found the ideal spot for a permanent base. It was on high ground; the jungle growth was low and easy to clear away. According to Lyle's map, it was not far from a Macurapi village. We spent a couple of days clearing out the jungle, pitching tents, and setting up camp. But we couldn't tarry as long as we wanted, for the rivers were already going down, and we had to get the boats out. The Abbeys, Lila, and the children remained, while Lyle, Ewart, and I began the long trek back to the rubber camp on Rio Colorado for another ferrying trip.

When we reached the house, we were pleased to find the rest of the provisions waiting which the Brazilians, by prearrangement, had ferried to us through the swamps from the mouth of Rio Mequenes. Also, there was a letter handed to me from Edith.

Dear Sweetheart:

I'm on my way downriver to Guajara Mirim and on to Cochabamba. Gwendolyn has been very sick with dysentery. She's had it two weeks now and I'm getting awfully worried, because she's lost a lot of blood.

This boat is stopping at the mouth of Rio Mequenes, so hope you get this letter. Poor little thing! How thin she is!

But I'm committing her into His care and praying you're all right too. I'm feeling fine.

Wish I could write a longer note, but there's not time. The boat is about ready to pull in to this place at Rio Mequenes.

With all my love,
Edith

How often I had to undergo these severe testings! Only the year before, Edith had been very sick with typhoid fever. One day her temperature had neared the fatal point of a hundred and seven. Prayer had saved her that time, and I could only trust God to do it again.

Despite unnerving news, there was work to be done. We had four weeks left in which to ferry in a tremendous load of supplies.

I wondered whether our outboard motors would hold out. They had already taken a real beating. One day, on the way through the Rio Terebinto, our brand new ten-horsepower outboard had caught on a vine. The momentum of the boat, loaded with a ton of supplies, had pulled the two-inch vine and the motor in a terrific tug-of-war until the whole framework of the motor tore apart. Of our three remaining smaller motors, one was out of commission with a broken shaft, and the other two had damaged slip-clutches from constantly hitting underwater objects. Fortunately, we were able to patch up these two enough to keep them going; but they were far from being in perfect running order, and we could only pray they didn't fail us.

Since the Sharps and Abbeys would be staying so many months, every ounce of provisions was needed. We would be unable to get anything in to them after the water went down. Ewart, Lyle, and I worked feverishly, loading the cargo. When we reached the Rio Terebinto, the water had lowered so far that a huge new tangle of logs was exposed. Besides, a storm had blown new trees across the river. Some of them were too big to cut through, so we had to unload our dugout, sink it, shove it under the logs, bail it out and load up again, only to repeat the process. All in all, we managed four trips in the six weeks. Then Ewart and I returned to Cafetal.

I spent several weeks at home base, enjoying the fellowship of the Sadlers and awaiting my family's return. I was overjoyed when I saw Edith, Connie, and Gwendolyn come off the mail boat. Two thousand miles round trip to reach a doctor! Gwendolyn looked fit as a fiddle and about twice as big as she had been when I last saw her; after all, she had been only a few days old then—now she was nearly three months. What a pleasure it was to relax for awhile, enjoy the family again, and catch up on all the news from Cafetal and the States.

12

Perilous Hours and the Inner Voice

As the weeks slipped by, I began thinking again about the Sharps and the Abbeys. Life must not be so easy for them at this moment. I found myself more and more preoccupied with thoughts of their welfare. Were their provisions holding out all right? We had lost a lot when the canoe sank. Were the medical supplies enough for any emergency? An inner voice kept telling me they were in need of me. Ewart and I spoke of a number of trips we might make to other tribes. We were anxious to plan new expeditions. But my desire to help others, and to place my own plans second, kept weighing on my mind. Even after days and days of inner struggle, I couldn't rid myself of the feeling that I had to go to them, though I didn't relish the thought of trying to get through the swamps— it might be impossible. It was the first week of September when I discussed it with Edith. She, too, felt I should go.

The swamp was now reaching its lowest level, the point at which it might be possible to get through it on foot. Ewart and I decided to try. We packed the foodstuffs and mail in small, rubberized bags.

The rains often begin in September, and the first storms are the fiercest. At the last moment an urgent feeling came over me: we should take along a lot of penicillin. We packed in enough to give one person daily shots for a month.

It took most of the first day to canoe downriver from Cafetal to the mouth of the Rio Mequenes. The following day, our packs strapped to our backs, we started across it by foot. The first part, we knew, would be the worst. And we could hardly have imagined it worse than it turned out to be. The thick black muck extends to an unknown depth—in the boats we had tested it with the fifteen-foot poles and pushed them all the way in without reaching bottom. Since the rubber workers occasionally venture through the muck, for a distance of perhaps two city blocks they have tied logs from one thorny palm tree to the next as an aid in getting across. We found these logs covered by about an additional foot of mucky water. We used a six-foot stick with a crotch on its end with which to probe and guide us over the sunken, slimy trail. Balancing was very difficult, for the logs were so slippery and insecure. In places like this we wear light tennis shoes. On dry ground we find heavy work shoes give us more comfort and protection.

The going was getting tough, when I heard a splash behind me. I didn't dare turn at once for fear of losing my balance. I got to the next tree as quickly as I could and looked back. Ewart was up to his chest in the mire. Desperately, he clawed at a log to keep from sinking deeper. The heavy pack on his back threw him off balance. I watched with horror as he struggled to get up onto the log. If he lost his hold, he would be finished. He worked frantically, clawing, slipping back, clawing harder, slipping again. There was nothing I could do. I knew if I added my weight to his on the log I would only add to his danger. If I tried to pull him out, he would surely pull me in. Finally—miraculously—he made it. He crouched there for a long moment, trembling and panting, before he inched forward to me. Then he stood hugging the thorny tree in thanksgiving. I could see how badly shaken he was.

"Bruce," he said, "it's too much. I hate like anything to say this, but I guess I'd better turn back. I can't go on."

The perspiration rolled down our faces. We looked at each other. Ewart could go no farther—no question about that. But should I give up and return with him? Or should he go back by himself while I pressed on alone? Common sense told me this was folly. In case of a mishap, death was almost certain for one alone, whereas with two there was always hope.

We said nothing, but set about dividing our food. This was not easy, as there was no place to put down our packs. Ewart took a step, then another, his weary body slumped forward under his pack. As I watched him go I still wasn't certain in my mind that I was doing the right thing. I could not bear another death. I was about to call to him to wait, when an inner voice spoke to me, saying, "No. You are needed. Go where you are needed." I watched wordlessly while Ewart's figure receded into the distance. When he was nearly hidden by the trees, he turned. We waved good-by—for the last time?

I plodded ahead into the swamp. An awful loneliness came over me—the loneliness that assails one who knows that nature is lying in wait, ready to resist any intrusion with all its weapons. I prayed for strength.

My mind played unkind tricks on me. I recalled Don Juan's story of the man who, thinking he knew the jungle well, went out hunting alone. Venturing farther than he realized, he lost his way. For days he wandered; bits of fruit partially sustained him, but his strength gradually ebbed away. He was indomitable, however. Patiently, patiently, despite his flagging energy, he sought a way out. Ninety days after he went in, he found it. He came stumbling into a settlement—and died.

I kept thinking that if I lost my way once I had made it out of the swamp, I could walk for miles in any direction and find nothing but solid jungle or uninhabited grasslands. Suppose my compass failed me? I wished that, like the missionary, I had three. My thoughts went to Ewart. I wondered what he was doing now, whether he was making it.

A few hours later I came to dry land. Compass in hand, I set off in a zigzag course, looking for the narrow trail the Indians and rubber workers use. I found it shortly. How strange it is that a homely, insignificant little path in a sticky grassland can be so beautiful—for it can mean life or death.

Trudging across the grassland, I came to the edge of the jungle where a rubber worker and his family had their camp. They asked me to stay the night with them. I gave them some of my provisions, and they gave me a dinner of rice and beans. I asked if it were possible to secure a guide to help me get through the cobweb of rubber trails feeding into the Indian trail beyond. The Brazilian was unable to leave his work and there was no one else in the neighborhood. I had the map Lyle had sketched for me, but it was rough, with directions left to guesswork at many points. I pored over it carefully, extracting from it as much as I could.

Bright and early the next morning, I thanked the rubber worker and his family and set off again. They showed me the trail that would lead to another rubber camp about fifteen miles away. Before long I reached a maze of several old rubber trails. They criss-crossed one another endlessly, doubled back, split apart. I set out on a likely-looking path, making trail blazes by hacking bark from the trees. The path turned and twisted, crossing many others. I kept on what I assumed was the main one, as far as I could tell, chopping as I went. I figured the curves to the right and the left eventually would lead me in the general direction I wanted to go.

But it was not long before I was encountering my own blazes again. How deceptive the trails were. I tried to be patient. I kept at it, trying one route and then the other that seemed to be the main trail leading in the right general direction. But every trail I tried seemed to turn back on itself or get lost in a maze of others. I became panicky. I hacked away, in my desperation, making ever bigger blazes. By the end of the afternoon, I succeeded only in coming full circle back to where I had started out that morning. This so discouraged me that I made up my mind to get a good night's sleep and then head for home.

Up at the crack of dawn, I felt relieved by my decision. Well, hadn't I made a good try? What more could anyone ask? It was obviously futile to go on wandering in circles.

I built a fire and got out the oatmeal. While it was cooking, I packed up my hammock and other supplies. In the pack I came across some of the extra penicillin I had brought along for the Sharps and Abbeys. The sight of the ampules brought me up short. I thought, "Suppose one or the other of them needs it? Perhaps it would be Lila, as she was to have given birth a month before, in August. Suppose they are praying and hoping at this moment that I show up to help them?"

My oatmeal was ready. I put these thoughts out of my mind. I was tired of this useless struggle. But the inner voice would not let me rest. As the warm, nourishing cereal filled me, I began to feel that if I turned back now I would be trading spiritual duty for physical comfort. The crowning argument came: I thought again of Dave and his tragic death. No counterarguments could hold water in the face of the power this thought still held over my conscience.

I headed in again. I was determined to keep in a straight line, no matter what. I decided to use my compass. If the trail deviated I would start making my own. I made huge blazes now so that they would be distinguishable from the previous ones. And this time I no longer went in circles. An unseen hand guided me: I found the right paths and *did* move more or less in a straight line. Before very long I was out of the maze of rubber trails and onto the clearer Indian trail. I followed this until about four in the afternoon, when a big storm came up. I stopped and crawled inside my waterproof jungle hammock to wait it out. I munched on a handful of sugar and a few raisins to quell my hunger. It was a violent storm: trees crashed down all around me. I did not bother with supper. In the early part of the night, as the storm continued, a small one of perhaps three inches in diameter fell across the lower part of the canopy. Water began to seep in. I was wet up to my knees and stayed that way for the rest of the night as I slept fitfully.

Three more days of trail blazing, getting lost, becoming more exhausted . . . Each night I would be determined to go back, but the inner voice urged me on.

Water was harder and harder to find. My thirst only added to my overall weariness. As I plodded down the trail, the packstraps digging into my shoulders like two vises, I began to feel as though I were on an endless, overgrown treadmill—each minute like the last, each hour like the last, each day like the last. Time, even the movement of the sun, was losing its meaning. One little clearing was like another, the towering trees covering all with their protecting, stifling, green ceiling.

The clacking, hungry jaws of seventy black wild pigs jerked me to my senses. I was standing in the middle of the grove of fat, moldering palms. The pigs had me surrounded, their white tusks glinting in the dappled jungle light.

I inched forward. The pigs in front of me moved back slightly.

I looked behind me. The rear guard of pigs had moved up with me. All around the circle, the hideous black beasts clacked away, unfazed by my movement.

They had me.

I had tried waiting them out long enough. The nine shots in my pistol, which I held in my trembling, perspiring right hand, were of little value, I knew. I had to try something more. So I took one clear, bold step forward.

The entire circle moved with me again—exactly as far as I had moved.

I did it again.

They moved again.

I wiped my brow. Perhaps, I thought, if I kept this up, I would reach the edge of the clearing where the tall trees were climbable. It was small hope—I couldn't stay in the tree forever—but it was temporary safety at least. I took another step. They followed. Another. They followed.

Now I was actually moving in a very slow walk, and they were moving along with me. Ever so gradually, I increased my speed. As

I did this, a strange thing began to happen. They increased theirs to a certain point, and then would go no faster, although I knew they were surely capable of it. Instead, as my speed continued to increase, the phalanx directly in front of me slowly parted, leaving a channel for me to walk through. As I approached, it widened. With steeled nerves, I continued on at the same even pace I had attained—right between the front rank of clacking pigs, like a general passing in review, their vicious incisors ten feet to either side of me like presented white sabres.

A minute later the last pig was behind me. Since I realized I had better continue to behave predictably, I kept up a steady pace and did not look back. I was in the denser jungle again. My mouth was absolutely dry, but the palms of my hands were so wet with fear that my pistol was slippery to the touch. The unbearable clacking continued behind me. I was afraid they might be massing for an attack from the rear, but I was equally afraid to look back. I kept increasing my pace.

Eventually their awful sound began to fade behind me, and I broke into a run. My heavy pack jolted up and down on my aching shoulders, but it was worth it to get away from them. My hands trembling, I put the safety catch back on and stuffed the pistol in my holster as I ran.

When I could hear that awful clacking no longer, I ran off the trail. Exhausted to the point of nausea, I tumbled to the ground. The pack flopped to my side and I slipped out of the cruel straps. I could feel a numb ache spreading from my back up my neck and through my whole skull. Every throb of my heart pounded the pain through my head. But there was release in that ache, the release from tension and fear.

I lay there in a state of semiconsciousness.

When I got to my feet, I had no idea how much time had gone by. A break in the ceiling of towering treetops revealed only light-gray clouds. Where was the sun?

Dizzily, I looked around me, trying to orient myself. I saw the trail from which I had spun off. Before shouldering my pack, I stood there in the tangled vines for a moment of reverence. I thanked Him for making the pigs give way and for saving my life.

I walked on and on. The light was fading. In another hour I found myself going in circles again, and paused to study my compass. Suddenly, coming in my direction down the trail, I saw an Indian. Behind him were several others. I hobbled toward them, smiling and holding out my arms in a gesture of friendship. I hadn't seen them before so didn't know if they were Macurapi Indians or another tribe which lived farther in. I said "good morning" in Macurapi (I had learned a few expressions from Lyle) and stepped to one side to allow them to pass. They muttered something and kept on. The direction from which they came was the general direction in which I wanted to go. I followed the ruffled leaves that indicated their zigzag path. Strange, I thought, that they didn't stop to find out who I was or what I was trying to say to them. The least they could have done was to indicate in sign language that they didn't understand me. Their manner had aroused my suspicions. They acted as if they were hiding something, as if they were afraid to speak to me, perhaps from some sort of guilt.

As I went on, the clouds were growing heavier and blacker. Before long it was raining. About three in the afternoon I came to the spot where the Indians must have camped the night before. Some hot coals glowed still, under a palm-leafed lean-to. It was raining hard now, and I was tempted to stop and make camp there for the night. Still, I reasoned, there were three hours of daylight left. I was very tired, but doggedly, I went on. A little farther ahead, the trail became hard to follow; after a bit, I lost it altogether. I spent the next two hours looking for it, gave up, and returned to the camp. To my joy, the coals were still glowing red; I could build a fire. My feet were the sorest they had ever been in my life. The wet work shoes had stretched, allowing my feet to slip and slide as I stepped over the roots and branches which cover the jungle floor. The skin was becoming terribly raw from breaking blisters. I was completely worn out. I lay in the hammock for half an hour, groaning. If crying would have relieved my sore feet, cramped legs, and shoulders aching from the heavy pack, I would have cried. I managed to push myself out of the hammock and boil some rice and dried soup. It took all the strength I had to perform such a simple task, but it was well worth it: nothing ever tasted more delicious. The Rio Terebinto was only a few yards away from the trail at this point. I would have dearly enjoyed a bath, but after lying down I was so sore and stiff that to walk even the few yards would be torture, so I just rolled back into the hammock.

I was awakened by the chorus of birds. The rain had stopped. I yawned and sat up. Then I stepped out of the hammock. I let out a howl, for my raw and blistered feet gave an excruciating protest. With much pain, I managed to get them into my socks and shoes, which were still wet. Then I slipped into my tattered, cold, wet shirt. I yawned again and sat on the hammock, recalling the frightful pigs and difficult trails of yesterday. I prayed nothing like that would happen to me today. The thought of hefting on my pack again and marching even one more hour filled me with revulsion.

I tottered to the fire and began cooking breakfast. The good smell revived my spirits a little. I reminded myself that if I pushed hard today I might be able to make it to the Sharps and Abbeys by nightfall. What with my feet, this might be pretty hard to do. Again, I was driven on by the feeling that they needed me. I had never known such urging as this before.

I rolled up my hammock and put everything away. When I lifted the pack onto my shoulders, stabs of weariness and pain cut my shoulders and back. Like an arthritic old man, I hobbled out onto the trail. Please, I prayed, no more going in circles, no more losing the trail! I had no energy to spare.

But again I had a hard time following it. I finally gave up the idea. With the compass, I struck out on my own in the general direction of the river, hoping that it might guide me to where the Sharps and Abbeys lived. It was rougher going, and my feet fairly screamed with soreness as I crashed through the jungle growth.

Still, it was better than walking in circles. In about two hours I ran onto the Indian trail again. It was clearly visible here, and I was able to pick my way along it. The sky began turning dark, then darker and darker. About noon it began raining again. I was almost in a trance. I longed to stop and rest, but I didn't dare. I knew if I stopped my muscles would stiffen up and I wouldn't be able to go on at all. I seemed to be moving through a dream world. My legs worked automatically. Tree after tree went by. From time to time the ground swam under me, and I had to jerk myself back to consciousness. My only thought was to get to the Sharps and Abbeys: get there, get them the penicillin, relax, sleep . . .

I stopped with a shock. Hanging all by itself from the limb of a tree in front of me was a packsack. It had a familiar look. I recognized the stains: no question—it belonged to the Abbeys.

What could this possibly mean?

I looked all around in the rain-soaked jungle. I listened—there was only the steady drip-drip of the rain on the leaves. If they had gone off the trail for some reason, Wilbur would surely not have left his pack hanging on a tree this way. Something unusual must have taken place. In country like this, that meant something had gone wrong. I dropped my pack. It hit the muddy ground with a splash. I opened the flap of the Abbeys' pack. It was full: clothes, powdered milk, oatmeal, a blanket. The powdered milk meant the baby was with them. It was inconceivable they would have just gone off and left all this. My heart sank with grief. Not death again! The whole family! I wondered whether I would be able to endure another tragedy such as Dave's. I literally didn't think I could. Impulsively, I looked around for their bodies. No sign of them anywhere.

Then I remembered the Indians and the furtive guilt with which they had passed me, their hurry to get away. *Had they murdered the Abbeys?* My mind, already numb with fatigue and grief, reeled. Only one piece of evidence dissuaded me from this belief: would the Indians have left the pack where it could be found?

I was getting a chill from standing in the rain. Stiffness was coming on, too. I'd better go on. How much farther could it be? Time had lost its dimension; I looked at my watch. Two more hours of daylight remained. I left the Abbeys' pack where it hung, wearily shouldered mine again, and stumbled on.

A few more miles down the trail I thought I smelled smoke. That could mean I was near camp. The prospect excited me. I pushed on at a clip that agonized my whole body. The smell of smoke grew more real. Lumbering on down the trail, I saw a clearing.

I was there!

But it appeared to be deserted. There was no sign of life around the shacks.

"Anybody home?" I called. My heart was in my throat.

Out of one of the huts came Lyle. "Bruce! Hey! Bruce is here! What a sight for sore eyes!"

I dropped my pack; we hurried toward each other and embraced affectionately.

"Where are the Abbeys?" was the first thing I asked.

Lyle's jaw dropped. "Didn't you see them?"

"No."

"They left here two days ago with seventeen Indians. They are returning to Cafetal and plan to go on back to Guajara Mirim. You should have met them on the trail."

Lila came running up and we embraced.

"I saw the Indians," I said, "but not the Abbeys."

Both of them looked alarmed.

"The Abbeys weren't with them?" Lila gasped.

"They could have been somewhere on the trail behind," I said, "because I lost my way right after that." I avoided telling about the pack at this point because I didn't want to upset them.

"That's probably it," Lyle said. "Boy, you look like a drowned rat."

Their little boy came running to greet me. "Hi, John Allen!" I caught him up in my arms.

"You're *dirty*!" he said.

I laughed. I hadn't thought about it until he mentioned it, but undoubtedly I was. I had been on the trail for ten days. My clothes were badly ripped, and I was soaking wet from head to toe. The rain was still coming down.

"Come on in and see our baby and get cleaned up," Lila smiled.

The baby was going on two months old now, fat and healthy.

"Life out here must agree with you people," I said. "I was worried about you and thought I'd better check."

Supper was ready. After eating, I lay on the hammock while Lila bandaged my blistered, infected feet. Lyle and Lila were full of questions and so was I. I finally told them about the Abbeys' pack.

"I can't imagine that anything serious could have happened," Lyle said. "The Macurapis have been quite friendly. Still, I don't understand it." They shared my concern. "I'll send a party of Indians out first thing in the morning to see if they can find out what happened."

In spite of my fatigue, I had a hard time getting to sleep. I noticed the Sharps' lantern was still burning. They were reading the mail I had brought them. After receiving none for eight months, they found it a great event, I knew.

Morning dawned bright and clear: the rain was over. Several Indians were around; one of them offered to wash my clothes. Another took my hammock and blanket out into the sun to dry. Lyle spoke to them, and a party set out to find the Abbeys. The camp had been made into a pleasant, homelike place. Right around the house some trees had been left for shade. Off a way was a nice patch of corn just coming up. "Boy, planting that sprouting corn really saved us," Lyle said. "It came into ear just as the rice was gone. This is our second crop."

Lila laughed. "Want any recipes for new ways to cook corn?" she said. "I've tried them all."

What a joy it was to rest all day! The closest I came to work was to offer a few comments on the next year's food order and supply list, which Lyle and Lila were making out for me to take back. As Lyle unpacked my pack for me, he came upon the supply of penicillin.

"I put in some extra; I had a feeling you might be needing it."

"Well, that's very kind of you, lugging it all that way for us. Of course we haven't used much of what we brought, but you never know." I could tell he thought the amount was a little excessive. He would later have cause to think otherwise.

The Macurapis returned in a couple of days. They had found no trace of the Abbeys, although they had brought back their pack. I couldn't get my friends off my mind. During the four days of rest Lyle showed me the large three-by-five card file that contained hundreds of Macurapi words and phrases. I was amazed they had been able to make progress.

The relaxation and warm fellowship had done me a world of good. My feet were in much better shape and the ache was gone from my muscles. My step was light as I retraced the route I had followed getting in. It was not hard to find now, for I had made big trail blazes in the difficult spots. Where I had been lost before, I now laughed, for I had blazed some of the trees as many as three or four times; their great size gave some indication of the mounting frustration and frenzy I had experienced as I went around in circles. But my heart was heavy. I looked and looked for some sign of the Abbeys—but I saw none. On the afternoon of the second day, the rheumatism in my knee, which had bothered me off and on ever since coming to Cafetal, flared up. It made each step an agony. It was scarcely better the next morning, but as I pushed on, the sheer effort took my mind off the pain.

Toward evening, I thought I heard a rooster crow in the distance. This was a welcome sound, indeed: it must mean I was approaching the rubber worker's hut where I had spent the night almost two weeks earlier. Here was my first chance to learn something about the Abbeys, I hoped: whether or not they had come this way. Perhaps I would even learn their reason for leaving the pack behind. But a wave of apprehension passed over me as I neared the house: if the Abbeys *hadn't* been seen by the rubber worker, then they might be lost—or dead—somewhere in the jungle behind me.

I reached the clearing. My heart leaped for joy. For a moment I thought my overwrought senses were deceiving me. Then I saw beyond a doubt. The couple sitting placidly in their hammocks under the thatched roof were most certainly the Abbeys! I hobbled toward them, speechless.

"Praise the Lord, there's Bruce!" Dorothy burst out. They both jumped to their feet and ran toward me, and we met in a three-way embrace.

"How long have you been here?" I asked, struggling out of my gear with Wilbur's help. "I saw your pack hanging on the tree there just a little way this side of the camp and I was really worried about you guys. What happened?"

Just then, the wife of the Brazilian rubber worker came out with a cup of their strong coffee and, beaming, handed it to me. After sipping a bit we began to walk toward the house to relax in the hammocks.

"Well," Wilbur resumed, "we wanted to go out because of our conference and to be with our two girls during school vacation. We were told that October was the time the swamp is the driest, so we thought we could make it. Those Macurapis were going out to get some supplies, so we persuaded them to act as our guides, and to carry some of our stuff, too."

"That's what Lyle told me," I said. "So what happened? I passed the Indians on my way in, but I didn't see you."

"Well, you know how those guys buzz through the jungle. They had to keep down to our pace, and after awhile they lost patience and said they couldn't wait for us. They told us we could easily follow their trail. Then they took off."

"Find their trail!" I exclaimed. "I wasted days and days looking for it."

"That's what happened to us," Dorothy said. "We couldn't find it, either."

"And the worst part was they just dumped all our stuff right there. We couldn't begin to carry it. And there was Timmy, too, you know; we had to take turns carrying him. So the only thing we could do was leave most of our food—that was the pack you found—and hope to shoot some wild game along the way. But pretty soon we were completely lost. We kept going in circles the way you did. We didn't know how much longer we could hold out."

"And then," Dorothy interrupted, "we ran across some of those blazes on the trees. There was only one guy we knew who made blazes like that, and they were fresh."

"Those blazes were like a superhighway," Wilbur said. "All we had to do was follow it right to the farm."

We reached the house and sat down in the hammocks. Their boy, Timmy, was asleep in one of them.

"Seriously, Bruce," Wilbur said, "those blazes saved our lives. Believe me, we would never have made it out without them."

"It's a fact," said Dorothy. "We were almost on the point of giving up."

I understood now why, on those days when I had gone in circles so many hours, the Lord had urged me to go on and on, in spite of the instinct for self-preservation that kept pressing me to return. I thanked Him for reminding me of the "second mile" principle, and for saving me from a fatal mistake that would have weighed on my conscience forever.

The next day dawned with the typical jungle haze. The sun, pushing its way through the trees, cast its light like a window into a dark, dusty room. Thanking our hostess with all the Latin-American courtesy we knew, we pushed on. We had to hurry, for the dry season was rapidly coming to an end.

After days of trudging with the heavy packs, we reached the edge of the swamp. There a rubber worker, who happened to be going through at the same time, offered to guide us. Late in the afternoon of the following day, we reached the Rio Mequenes. Our energy was just about completely gone by this time. Suddenly I let out a whoop of joy. There was Ewart, walking slowly up to meet us. He had made it! This was the first I knew for sure that he was alive and safe.

The following day we went by dugout canoe to Cafetal. I don't think I was ever happier to see anyone more than Edith. She was equally happy to see me. I sank into our beautiful mud hut for a long rest, and she began the usual task of trying to put fat back onto my ribs. (I generally lose about a pound a day when hiking with a heavy pack.) The Abbeys left in a few days for Guajara Mirim.

After they had gone we were looking at old snapshots, and little Connie pulled one out of the pile. It was a photograph of a skinny, bearded figure with tattered clothes, tape wrapped around bare toes which protruded through rotted shoes, and a sad face—a picture Edith had taken of me the day I arrived back from the long trip. I had developed the film.

Connie looked up at Edith. "What dat, Mommy?" she said.

It was January, 1954, the middle of the rainy season and three months after the Abbeys went downriver to Guajara Mirim. We were expecting the Sharps any time now. My ears were usually half-cocked for the hum of Lyle's outboard motor.

At suppertime one day I jumped up from the table. "Sounds like Lyle's motor!" I exclaimed. Edith and I rushed to the river-bank. We were overjoyed to see the Sharps pull up to the shore. Lyle moved slowly and looked haggard.

Lila explained: "About a month ago Lyle began getting a severe pain in his appendix. I began giving him shots of penicillin every day. We just used up the last that you brought in to us."

"You come just at the right time," I said, "for the mail boat is upriver and should be back in a couple of days. It will be a week before you can get to the hospital in Guayaramerin, so you'd better take some of the penicillin we have left and continue taking the shots."

Upon returning a couple of months later, Lyle said, "Bruce,

the doctor in Guayaramerin told me that if it hadn't been for the penicillin, I wouldn't be here. Surely the Lord must have guided you to make that trip during the dry season to bring in that big supply."

How glad I was again for that persistent inner voice!

13

A New Front:
Commandos for Peace

The sun climbed over the mountain peaks like a misty orange ball, the same sun the Incas had once worshiped right there in the Cochabamba valley where Tom Moreno and I stood. The mountain air was chilly. Where an ancient temple might once have been, we waited near the runway for our supplies to be loaded onto the plane.

It was the dawn not only of a new day but of an era of new experiences for us. Watching the deep purple shadows give way to the advancing rays of the sun, I thought: "How fast time goes by; how quickly events change our lives." It was December, 1955. Tom Moreno and I were going on a mission together for the first time after having been separated for four years. When he had finally returned to Cafetal with an injunction from the government to keep the rubber workers away from the Nhambiguaras, it was too late. Dave was already dead. And with the contact at an end, Tom had returned to Cochabamba and had gone out from there to other areas. He had married an American missionary soon after leaving.

182

The couple were living in Cochabamba with their two children.

As for us, Edith and I and the children: we had gone to the States in May, 1954, for our year's furlough after seeing the Macurapi work get off to a successful start. We had recently returned to Cochabamba.

Again I had to wait as I considered where I might be needed most, or whether to begin a new contact of my own. My answer came in an urgent telegram from a fellow missionary in Todos Santos:

INDIANS MOVED INTO AREA. FARMERS KILLED SEVERAL. NEED HELP DESPERATELY. LES FOSTER.

Tom and I were soon on our way, sorry to leave our families but glad to be doing God's work. Todos Santos, fairly new to missionaries, was a settlement of about fifteen hundred people northeast of Cochabamba, about a forty-five-minute flight over the Andes. Aloft in the clear air, I watched the Todos Santos road twist its serpentine way over the steep, forested slopes below. Here and there a banana truck crawled over it like a tiny insect. Half an hour after takeoff, the mountains dropped sharply. In another fifteen minutes we were over flat jungle lowlands. We landed in Todos Santos.

Lois Foster was at the grass airstrip to meet us. As we walked toward her home, I asked her where Les was.

"He's out with Bob Wilhelmson, trying to contact the Yuquis," she said. I shuddered at the thought, for both the Fosters and the Wilhelmsons were fairly new in the field and lacking in missionary experience. Bob, in his early twenties, was filled with youthful enthusiasm.

"How do we find them?" I asked Lois.

"You go upriver about fifteen miles to where you'll see several scattered farms. From there you go down a path, I think for maybe a mile. You pass about three farmhouses, then you come to one that's abandoned. That's where the fellows should be."

There was no time to lose. Within the hour we had found a

Bolivian who would take us up in his dugout, powered by an out-board. We covered the distance in about two hours. Then, our packs loaded, we hurried down the trail. We came across what seemed to be the abandoned farmhouse. It looked more like a temporary shelter. Four corner posts held up a palm-leafed roof. There were no upright poles for walls, so the simple, bamboo double bed had little protection from weather. We went inside, and saw Les and Bob's packs and hammocks. It was late afternoon. They should be in at any moment, so we sat down to wait for them.

The last time I had seen either of them was about a year and a half earlier, before we went on our furlough. I had first known Bob back in bootcamp in California, and met Les when he first came to the field.

Before long they appeared and we greeted each other warmly. One of the most satisfying aspects of missionary life is the lasting bond that develops between fellow workers.

"Man, am I glad to see you guys!" said Les. "We're really in a fix."

"We're going to need your help," said Bob. "Right now I'm starved. Let's have supper and then talk."

I noticed that Les was wearing a beard, the mark of the new man in the field. (I had grown one myself when I went out on my first expedition to the Sansimonianos.) The new missionary considers it a sign of his adaptability to life in the jungle. But more often than not he soon finds that shaving every day is a greater boost to his morale.

Les's beard seemed a slightly disturbing indication of naïve enthusiasm—the sort of zeal that might lead him into trouble. On the other hand, his calm confidence was reassuring. Les was at home in the out-of-doors. Raised on a farm in Iowa, he had spent some time in the mountains of the west. A bright metal belt buckle with the word "Colorado" on it in large, raised letters was his reminder of happy days spent in that state's rugged terrain.

Les walked the trail with rapid, impatient stride. But when it came time to make a decision, he would stand with his arms folded across his chest and his lips pursed in thought, thinking things through before he spoke or acted.

I was not surprised when I awoke one morning after we had been out in the jungle for several days to find Les had shaved off his beard.

Informally, we designated him as our chief, which was to help greatly in our contact with the Yuquis.

After supper we piled logs high onto the fire, for there was plenty to catch up on. I was full of questions. Les looked serious and intent, the very part of his nature. Perhaps his years in the service during the war and the start of raising a family of three children also had much to do with it. He leaned his tall, muscular body forward to push a log toward the center of the fire. Then he spoke:

"We've got a real problem on our hands," he said. "Just a few miles from here—back in the jungle—is this stone-age tribe they call the Yuquis. It isn't often you find such a primitive bunch roaming so close to an outpost of civilization. It's the chance of a lifetime to reach them with the Gospel—right now. This is the first time in fourteen years that they've showed up around here."

His dark eyes glowed with enthusiasm as he leaned down to poke up the fire.

"But there are a couple of little obstacles in the way that we've got to overcome first," he went on.

"Such as what?" I asked.

"Well, first we've got to bring an end to the war between the Yuquis and the Bolivian farmers before the tribe can be reached."

"What kind of war?" I wanted to know.

"Well, here's the situation," Les went on. "I'll tell you about the farmers first. They're about as miserable an underprivileged lot as I've ever seen. They live on little clearings right on the edge of the jungle where they raise hardly enough to feed themselves bananas, yucca, corn, and so on. What little cash they have they get from growing *coca*."

I knew about *coca*. It is a mild narcotic that Quechua Indians like to chew, and also others who look to it to relieve their misery.

"The farmers' existence was tough enough already," Les said. "Then a while back the Yuquis came here. No one knows why. The theory is that a flood must have driven them from their home in the lowlands, just as it did when they showed up the last time fourteen years ago. Up till that time the farmers' lives had been hard enough. But when the Yuquis started stealing their crops, they were faced with starvation."

"But what about the killing?" I asked.

"I was coming to that," Les said. "It was terrible. About two weeks ago, the farmers took matters into their own hands. To them, the Yuquis are wild animals; they consider them like the *tigres* who come and steal their chickens. They found a Yuqui camp about two miles west of here in the jungle and sneaked up on it. They caught the Indians by surprise—the men were all off hunting. Only the women and children were there. Some were weaving baskets, some making string for hammocks or to bind feathers to the arrows. The farmers started firing on the women. One fell; others grabbed their children and tried to flee. Blood spurted from their naked bodies as the farmers fired again and again. Nobody knows how many were killed. Some of the children stood there, paralyzed with fear. The farmers seized four of them and carried them off.

"The Indians must have heard the shots and raced for the camp. They ran after the Bolivians, shooting at them with arrows. One farmer got an arrow in the leg."

Bob picked up the story: "When the news reached us in Todos Santos, we were infuriated by the injustice of it. We sure felt sorry for those poor Indians."

"What became of the Yuqui children?" I asked.

"As far as we can learn, the farmers gave them to different families in Todos Santos to raise as servants," Les said.

"So what's happened since?" I wanted to know.

"We've been tramping around through the jungle, putting out gifts and trying to find the tribe," Les said.

My blood ran cold at the thought.

"But how do you know the Indians won't think you're on the farmers' side?" I demanded.

"We've thought of that," Les said, "but we never carry any guns, so they won't be scared."

"And we've been thinking about painting our gifts a different color," Bob put in, "so they won't think the farmers are setting a trap for them."

My mind went back to my own first days in the field. I remembered the risks we had taken in trying to make first contact with the Nhambiguaras, before we had learned how tricky and dangerous they were. I understood so well the earnest zeal of the new missionary, the eagerness to get on with the work. But I had also learned through experience, suffering, and tragic loss of the need to temper eagerness with patience and realistic caution.

"Look fellows, take it easy," I said. "We've got to face the fact that we're right in the middle of a war. And we've got to try to end it, before we can make any contact with the Yuquis."

"We're sure glad that you came down," said Bob somewhat sheepishly. "I guess we're kinda green at this."

"That's just what we've been thinking," Les said. "We know the farmers are mad, but they must be scared, too. If they keep up this shooting, the Indians are bound to try to get their revenge. Then there'll be more killings and more killings."

"So what's the answer?" I asked.

"To try to win the confidence of the farmers first—to get them to refrain from shooting—even if the Yuquis *do* steal their crops."

"If we can accomplish that, then we can try to win the friendship of the Yuquis," I said. "But in the meantime we'll have to go slowly. You fellows must realize the danger we're in. Why right here, right now—this fire in the middle of the darkness makes us a perfect target for their arrows. I don't mind telling you I'm a little bit jumpy."

Bob was looking seriously at the fire. He said, "I think I'll go home to mamma." We roared with laughter. Bob was a great joke-ster, a real asset in situations such as this. But he made his quips with a solemn face.

Les got up to put some water on for coffee. "You and Tom," he said, looking at me, "have had plenty of experience in contact work. So we'll go along with whatever you suggest."

I proposed a plan for laying a network of trails and putting out gifts, as we had done before with the Nhambiguaras.

"I can just see us, the way we were doing!" Bob exclaimed. "Why, even though we didn't have guns, the Yuquis would prob-ably think we were out to kill them. It's a good thing you guys came along, to calm us greenhorns down."

Tom and I were glad they saw this point. Naturally, we would have liked to make a friendly contact right away. Yet we knew we had to take our time. It would require months or even years of labor, sweat, trial, and fierce spiritual warfare before this tribe could be reached with the Gospel.

In the fading light of the fire, a wide shadow hovered over our heads. Huge vampire bats, with a wing span of a foot-and-a-half, swooped through the air, catching mosquitoes. As we tied up our jungle hammocks for the night, we were glad for the mosquito nets. Poor vampire bats! We didn't give them a chance at our vitamin-enriched blood.

In the next few days we visited several farmers living in scattered clearings along a six-mile strip by the river. From our conversations with them, we learned they had a leader. We sought him out and found him friendly and approachable. He was short and handsome in a suave Latin-American way, with a neatly trimmed mustache, and dark wavy hair. He seemed more industrious than most. He was receptive to our plan and thought it would be a good idea if he called a meeting of all the farmers to deal with the situation.

The word went out. The meeting was to be held at the leader's farm, which was centrally located. The morning we arrived, the trees were still dripping from the morning dew. We were the first ones there. The farmers began to straggle in. Since we had visited among them, we recognized a few; but gathered together, how different they looked! They were like a ragged platoon left over from World War I. Some wore sandals, some were barefoot. We couldn't tell what part of their shirts and trousers was a patch or what part was original. Their appearance was the more forbidding because many hadn't seen a razor for weeks. Their cheeks bulged with great wads of *coca* leaves; their teeth and lips were usually green from chewing it. All were carrying rifles that looked to be of pre-World War I vintage. Many of the guns had the old hexagon-shaped barrels of the beginning of the century. Some wore old, caved-in straw or felt hats; others came bareheaded.

As they drifted in, we missionaries sat on a log on the edge of a grassy patio. All around us were *coca* leaves spread out on canvases to dry.

Les murmured, "Just look at those guys! I surely can feel for them. It must be awfully rough making a living down here. What a plight! You *know* they needed every bit of that yucca, and that corn, and those bananas the Indians took."

The place was soon humming with excitement. About fifty farmers now stood around in small, sullen groups, talking heatedly. Arms flailed; lips protruded in angry speech.

"Boy, they're in no mood for reconciliation," Bob muttered.

"We've got to get their co-operation," said Tom with determination. "There are no two ways about it."

"They remind me of a bunch of hornets after a stone has been thrown through their nest," said Bob.

"Tom's right," I said, "but there's one thing we have to be careful about, above all."

Bob and Les looked at me expectantly.

"We mustn't appear to be taking the Yuquis' side. That'll throw these farmers off quicker than anything."

"Still," Les added quickly, "we've got to present the Indians' case. We're the intermediaries, carrying the messages of each side to the other, because they can't communicate directly."

"Right," I agreed. "This is very, very delicate. We've got to stay strictly in the middle. If we seem to slip off this thin line one way or the other, our cause is dead."

"And maybe us along with it," Bob said, his eyes sweeping over the surly farmers.

The meeting was called to order. Some of the farmers sat around on logs. Others just squatted on their haunches like Indians. They alternately chewed and spat.

The leader opened by asking for any questions the farmers wanted to direct to the missionaries.

One asked, "Why are you guys here, risking your lives? You think these savages have gold hidden somewhere?" He looked at the ground as he talked and, when he had finished, spat.

In Spanish, Tom spoke out. "Men, we're not here for money. If we wanted money and all the pleasures of the world, we'd have stayed in our own country. For instance Bruce, here, could be making thousands of dollars back in the States if he continued in his tree-surgery work. We're after something more precious than gold: *the souls of men*. See, men, in God's sight the souls of these Yuquis are just as precious as yours and mine. God's Word says 'all have sinned.' Jesus shed His blood to pay for their sins as well as for ours. Salvation is a free gift of God. We have come to offer this free gift even though it may cost us our lives."

They looked at us strangely. Most of them had never heard talk such as this before. Some stirred restlessly. The sun rose higher in the sky and began beating down on us. We answered a few more specific questions about who we were and what we wanted. Farmers in this area are suspicious, and live on the edge of disaster. But at least they were willing to stay and listen. They seemed set in their attitudes. They sat and squatted there implacably, the mosquitoes buzzing about their shaggy heads, their anger burning silently and slowly. Tom got up and gave a long sermon. It lasted over an hour. His purpose was twofold: not only was this a chance to do some evangelizing, but, perhaps more important at this point, the sheer passage of time would cool the farmers off and wear down their resistance.

Tom's remarks also forced the farmers to do a little reconsidering. He urged them to think in terms not only of war and survival but of spiritual accounting to God. He explained that since we were here to help them, if they so wished, I would be willing to go to La Paz to ask the government to compensate those among them who had suffered loss. If they would co-operate with us, he said we would try to establish a friendly contact with the Indians and get them to stop both the stealing and the shooting. Only then would the farmers' lives and property be safe. Tom thanked them graciously for their attention, and sat down.

The effect was sobering. There was a long silence. A few farmers coughed and shifted their weight on their doubled-up legs. Finally, the leader opened the meeting for further discussion.

One farmer stood up. In a measured monotone, he said, "I think we ought to go in and wipe out those good-for-nothing animals once and for all." He sat down. Another got up. "These missionaries ought to have their chance. What have we got to lose? Give them a little time and see what happens. Then we can meet again and decide."

The majority agreed to this. We felt it was at least a beginning. Yet, while we worked, would some of these farmers take it on themselves to shoot at the Indians and thereby endanger our lives?

Weeks went by—weeks of uneasy peace. I was asked to represent our Mission to the government and had to leave for an indefinite period. For months, the patience and endurance of my friends was sorely tested. They continued visiting the farmers as well as hiking miles every day over jungle trails to check on gifts for the Indians. None were taken. They worked hard at establishing contact with little success. Dick Strickler, a former astronomer with the U.S. Naval Observatory, and Harold Rainey, a former woodsman, joined the effort on a permanent basis. From time to time others went to help them for periods of a few weeks.

Discouragements piled up. Although the missionaries managed to hold the line against open warfare, no basic improvement was made in the situation. Then, after a whole year of labor, there came a real setback. A telegram from one of our men in Todos Santos reached me in Cochabamba:

BOLIVIAN WOMAN KILLED BY INDIANS. FARMERS GIVE US TWO WEEKS TO BRING MORE MISSIONARIES INTO AREA OR GET OUT.

Back I went immediately.

"Did you get anywhere with the officials in La Paz about obtaining more help for the farmers?" Les asked as I got off the plane.

"Yes, they promised all right, but I haven't seen either funds or food as yet."

"That's tough," Les said.

"I also got a permit from the government to take the kidnaped children away from the people in town that have them and return them to the Indians. But it's no good now. I had a check made on the whereabouts of these children. One family, for lack of work, moved to Argentina. Another couple with a Yuqui child moved to La Paz. If it proves impossible to get these two children, I don't know what we're going to do. I did see two of the older ones in Todos Santos when I left you guys the last time. It would be difficult even to get those, for the Bolivians are so attached to them by now."

We learned the farmers' leader had called a meeting for nine o'clock the next morning. When we arrived the sun was already hot. A number of them were preparing to go on a killing raid against the Indians. We found a few already there. We spoke to them, but they hardly had a civil word for us. As always, whenever we met them now, they carried their loaded guns in ready position.

"Since the killing they travel only in groups," Les explained. "A man alone could be too easily ambushed."

The meeting began; the air was heavy with threat. Man after man got up to demand that a raiding party be formed at once to attack the Yuquis. One protested to the others, "We've given these missionaries a whole year and they haven't done a thing. If you ask me, they're scared—scared of those animals. I say it's time to take matters into our own hands. I say it's kill first—or be killed."

A rumble of angry response indicated agreement. The simmering fury in their voices which I had noted a year before was reaching the point of explosion.

"Very well, *señores*," drawled the leader quietly. "You have spoken. Now let us hear what the missionaries have to say."

Les got up and spoke to them in Spanish. Standing with his feet spread apart and his arms folded when he wasn't making gestures, he radiated confidence. "Men, we have done everything in our power to contact the Yuquis. We have put out gifts; we have hiked hundreds of miles on dangerous trails so that we might bring them the Gospel and you and your families would be safe. It is true that we have failed, but we have tried. It is not our fault that your woman was killed. Now—have you thought of this—if you go in and kill even two or three of those Indians, then they will never stop until they have killed every one of you."

There was a slight mutter.

"And besides, you're going to have to give an account to God for each Indian you send off to eternity." Several eyes were looking down at the ground as if this were a new thought to them. Then the men started talking loudly among themselves.

A few more groups had come in. There must have been about ninety altogether. The leader paced slowly back and forth, seemingly struggling with the pros and cons of what he had heard. The argument reached a tumultuous pitch.

"Quiet, please," the leader said. "Quiet, please. We're going to take a vote. If you men vote to go in to kill, just make sure every man who voted goes in on the expedition. I don't want a man to back out. Think seriously how you vote. Don't be led by your emotions. All right, those of you who want to go in to kill, line up on this side of the patio." He pointed to one side. There was a scramble. It seemed as though most of the men were lining up there. Chewing their *coca* excitedly, now and then shifting the wad to the other cheek, they talked feverishly.

"Quiet, please. Now, the rest of you men who think this is foolish, line up on the other side."

The farmers began to divide, going in one direction or the other.

"Doesn't look too good for us, Les," I said.

He didn't seem to hear me. In about a minute he said, "What? What did you say?" I realized he had been praying.

"Never mind, Les." The leader was motioning for silence again, so I didn't want to miss what he was going to say.

The leader looked disappointed at the way the men were lining up. I guess he saw things our way. I hoped that he would exert some influence.

Fifty wanted to kill. Thirty-nine didn't. Every bit of our labor, sweat, tears, aching muscles, time spent—now it all seemed in vain. The leader kept the discussion going. He presented to the men the advantages of giving us more time. One farmer on the "kill" side said, "We live in fear all the time. We can't go nowhere or work none of our farms but what we could get shot any minute. Let's get it over with."

Another spoke up: "*Los salvajes* are out for revenge. Let's get them before they get us."

A silence followed. No one moved. The sun was beating down hard. Everyone was sweating and the farmers kept taking off their battered hats and wiping their foreheads. No air stirred.

Then one farmer spoke up in our defense. "Where does it get us? Kill and we get killed. The savages have lived in the jungle all of their lives. If we go in again, they won't be taken by surprise. The missionaries have a point. Give them a chance."

Another spoke up quickly. *"Si,"* he said. "If they are willing to risk their lives for our benefit, it's only right we try to help them."

These comments brought quick opposition.

"I say let's kill the good-for-nothing animals that killed Maria. Are you guys cowards?"

More discussion. "Very well, *señores*," the leader began again, wiping his brow. "I'm giving you one more opportunity to change your minds. If you want to change sides, this is your last chance."

There was a pause. One man stepped out of the "kill" side. Slowly, he walked across the yard to the other side. Our hearts were heavy. One didn't count for much. If only more would follow him. Then another stepped out. A pause. One more. We missionaries had our heads bowed, praying. But from under my eyelids I couldn't help watching. A few more stepped out. Then they stopped.

"Count again," said the leader.

I wiped my forehead. I could hear the faint hum of mosquitoes in the silence. My heart raced.

"*Muy bien, señores,*" the leader said. "Now we take the final count." He went down the first line, then the other, ticking off the numbers. Then he spoke.

"Forty-three to kill. But forty-six against. That's it—we do not go."

The lines broke up into groups. Some of the farmers were pleased; others cursed. To us, their decision meant everything. God had wrought a victory over their hearts. We were free to go on with our work.

In the next week we redoubled our efforts to make contact with the Yuquis. We put in ten hours a day hiking with gifts, or searching for new trails. With us it was now or never.

The Indians continued to steal from the farmers. While we worked in one area we would hear they had struck in another. And always they eluded us.

I received word that I was again needed to work with the government in Cochabamba. I arranged to keep in daily radio contact, and assured Les I would come back on a moment's notice in case of trouble.

Les had been holding the line at La Jota for several months when he sent for me.

"Well," I said when he and the other missionaries met me at the airstrip, "I see the Indians haven't put any of you in the soup kettle yet."

"Those Yuquis are fussy," Harold said with a grin, as he and Dick boarded the plane for a two-week rest in Cochabamba. "They're waiting for a lean slab of bacon like you."

As Don Hay, Paul Mason, Les, and I headed up the road, Les said, "The Indians finally took some gifts. We were hoping a friendly contact might be possible. Then the worst happened: the Yuquis shot a farmer. Not long afterward they killed another."

"How did you keep the farmers from total war?" I asked.

"I guess they were too demoralized to fight back," Les went on. "All the farmers around La Jota got so scared they moved away. But as soon as they left, the Yuquis burned down several of their houses. This made the farmers madder than ever."

We were at the house. After I greeted Lois, Les continued: "We were determined to reach the Indians, so we had a couple of houses built at La Jota and made our base right there. I brought Lois and the children out there to be with me. I thought if they saw I had a wife and children of my own, then they'd know we had no intention of stealing theirs. And it worked. At last we did make a friendly contact."

I looked at Lois and said, "You were a brave girl."

She let us know that supper was ready, and our conversation turned to other things. But I was too curious to let the subject drop. "What are the Yuquis like?" I asked.

Les chuckled. "We honestly don't know what to make of them—they're so unpredictable," he said. "One minute they're okay, playing around like kids. Then all of a sudden they'll show a mean streak and come right into our house while we're there and tear everything apart. Only a few days ago they smashed my radio, my transmitter, and my tape recorder. They took our food and poked holes in the cans of food they didn't take. After that they seem all right. What do you make of such characters?"

"Wow!" I said. "They must keep a guy on edge. Maybe we'd better have five or more men on the contact all the time. That just might calm them down."

"It got too risky to have Lois there, so I brought her and the children back to Todos Santos. We moved out of the area and just went back every few days to meet them. They always hung around La Jota, so usually we met them."

It was a solemn hour. I wondered if Les were fully aware of the chances he had been taking. As the most experienced of the group, I felt a great responsibility. With the experiences I'd had, and with the work the Spirit of the Lord had done in my life through the years, I was challenged anew to put it all to use, to give all I had, to salvage this work.

Conversation turned to future plans and tactics. Then, as the cool night air brought with it the symphony of frogs through the glassless windows, we went to bed. How precious fellowship is, I thought, when hearts are united in working toward the same objective.

Following an early breakfast, four of us—Les, Don Hay, Paul Mason, and I—started upriver. A light jacket felt good in the crisp, damp jungle air. After two hours in the dugout we came to a palm-thatched shack which one of the farmers used to store *coca*.

"Okay, fellows," Les said to us. "Off with your shirts and watches. Empty your pockets." He put our belongings in a barrel and locked the lid.

We checked over our gifts. Each of us had brought along either some sweetened condensed milk or a two-pound bag of sugar. Les even carried a live rooster under his arm. Then off we went. I struggled against the fear that was pressing in on me. I prayed—and soon found myself humming a hymn.

In a few hours we drew near La Jota. The hiking was easier; we were going along a broad path lined with banana trees. Here and there off to one side, we glimpsed a clearing with a farmhouse in the middle of it. Every one had been abandoned.

Suddenly Les stopped. "There they are!" he whispered excitedly.

At first we could see nothing. Then, from the spaces between the broad banana leaves, we saw brown faces peering out. A hush lay over the sun-splashed path. Presently it was broken by a low, mournful, whistling sound, like that of the mourning dove.

"They want to look us over before they come out," Les whispered.

Holding our hands up to show we were unarmed, we advanced slowly toward them. Cautiously, the Yuquis began to emerge from hiding. I counted about twenty—men, women, and children. They looked unlike any tribesmen I had ever seen. Their high cheekbones and long, straight noses suggested some relationship with the Indians of North America. Most of the Indians I had met so far in both Brazil and Bolivia had flat, broad faces, indicative of Mongolian origin. I was filled with wonder to think how they had survived here through the centuries.

Knowing nothing of the Yuqui background or temperament, I had no idea how to deal with them. But they were coming. I would have to learn as I had before, simply through experience.

As they approached, Les pointed out the ones to whom he had already given nicknames. First came "Roughneck," and then "Toughy." "Roughneck," with his big, bulging shoulders, flashing, restless black eyes, and quick, catlike movements, reminded me of a boxer. "Toughy" was more the wrestler type. Shorter and wider, he walked with his feet apart, on the alert, as though ready to spring. Behind them both came "Witchy," an undersized but crafty little man with long, stringy hair hanging down over his glassy eyes.

"We think he's the witchdoctor," Les said.

We had no trouble picking out the chief. He was tall, erect, and walked and spoke with an air of authority. A small, wispy goatee gave him a slightly comic look.

The men all carried their bows, which were about seven feet in length, as well as several long arrows. From their bulging chest muscles and biceps I gathered they must have had plenty of practice in using them. I made up my mind I'd think twice before trying to tangle with any of them. But it was their black eyes that impressed me the most. They were shifty, restless, always darting from side to side, on the alert for any sudden move.

They were all naked. The women had the oddest hairdos I had ever seen. They looked as though they had been half-scalped. Their heads had been shaved in a triangle that went down on either side from a topknot, giving the impression they were prematurely bald. Most of the men had painted their faces and chests a brilliant orange red. The rest of their bodies were covered with black ashes. Unlike the Nhambiguaras and Macurapis, who were darker skinned under their ashes, these Indians were nearly white. One lad in particular, about fifteen, who wore no paint, was nearly as white as we were. Les had nicknamed him "Joven" (Spanish for youth).

The women looked sorrowful and rather fragile, although I knew they must have plenty of stamina to survive their rugged nomadic life.

The Yuquis inspected us thoroughly, one by one. We could only hope they were feeling our muscles to see how tough we were— not, as we found out the Nhambiguaras had done, to see if we would make good eating. It wasn't long before we were as red as they.

The chief came up and said something to us.

"He wants everyone to take off his right shoe," Les said, and went on to explain that they were still looking for a foot to fit the print left by a farmer after he had killed one of the Yuqui women at a spot not far away. I tried to comfort myself by thinking that no Bolivian was likely to have a foot as big as mine. But all the same, this ritual was not exactly reassuring. What if they made a mistake? Nervously, I took off my number-ten work shoe, remembering I must not show fear. Looking down at my foot in the stone-age hand, I asked the Lord to see to it that the chief made an accurate judgment. After a minute or so, he motioned that I put my shoe back on. "Whew!" I thought to myself. "Crisis number one out of the way."

The Yuquis went through all our pockets and found nothing they wanted. Then Toughy spotted my wedding ring. He wanted *that* all right. I tried to persuade him, by pulling on it in vain, that it wouldn't come off. (Naturally I didn't let him know that I *could* get it off—with a lot of twisting and turning.) He gave the ring a determined yank. My knuckle snapped loudly. Then, convinced he couldn't get the ring off without taking my finger with it, he gave up in disgust.

At several places on the men's bodies, we noticed the pink-colored scars left by bullets. When they caught us looking at them, Roughneck and Toughy began, with much incomprehensible eloquence and many gestures, to recount the stories of how they had acquired them in their battles· with the Bolivians. As they spoke their faces grew more and more contorted with thirst for revenge.

This was making me feel queasy. Then, without warning, I felt myself seized from behind. Somebody was trying to throw me. Turning, I saw it was Roughneck. My first impulse was to defend myself, to try to throw my attacker. But I remembered Les's warning that we should struggle a little at first, just enough to show we weren't weak, then let the Indians throw us in the end. If any of us won, the Yuquis would get furious and start beating us up. (Les had found this out the hard way.) After I struggled for a bit with Roughneck, I let him throw me. The fall shook me all over. But I found nothing was hurt but my ego. His, on the other hand, was inflated.

In sign language, Les indicated the time had come for us to head back to Todos Santos. Motioning to the sun and sweeping his arms from east to west, then shutting his eyes and giving a snoring sound—and repeating it all twice—he indicated the passing of three days and three nights. Then, pointing to the position of the sun at ten o'clock in the morning, he conveyed the idea that we would meet them on this very spot three days from now.

We took a step or two to leave. The women came up and stood before us, blocking our path. One, whom we took to be the chief's wife, was the leader.

They said something to us, or rather made noises at us. When we showed them by signs and by shrugging our shoulders that we did not understand, they burst into hysterical weeping. Then they came up to us, gesturing more violently than before. Frail as they were, the women seemed capable of more violent emotion than the men. We wanted to leave; they barred our path. We were wondering what move we could possibly make next when the chief barked an order. The women stepped aside and let us go.

Once back on the trail, we talked about this new development. Now we had the unpredictability of the women as well as of the men to deal with.

"Why do you suppose the women are so mad at us?" Don asked. "We haven't done anything to them."

"All I can think of is that they're expecting us to bring their children back," said Les.

"If that's true, we're in for trouble," I said, "because at the moment I don't see how we're going to manage it."

Our conversation turned to the brighter side of the contact. Except for the anger of the women, things had gone well—better than we might have expected.

Three days later we were again on the trail on our way toward the appointed spot. Our hopes were high. We had decided to press our success; we would take advantage of their good behavior the last time and try to start getting the upper hand. One way we had in mind was to deny them something—so I left my shirt on.

We had brought a camera along for the first time—a cheap one, a box Brownie, that might at least give us a recognizable picture, yet would be no great loss should the Indians steal it. Later, if we were able to photograph them with this one, we would try a more expensive 35mm. camera with which we could take color slides.

As we neared La Jota, we fell silent. We rounded a bend and stopped, aghast. Directly before us, a farmer's house was burning fiercely.

"What do you think, Les?" I said uncertainly. "It doesn't look like they're in a mood for a friendly contact."

"Boy, it doesn't look too good. Maybe we'd better—" Les's words were cut short by that long, mournful whistle.

"This is it," someone said. There was no changing our minds now.

Ceremonially, we held up our hands to show we were carrying no guns. Next, we laid down our gifts.

A few heads appeared from behind clusters of banana trees, glancing around curiously. Very cautiously, and one by one, the Indians came out of hiding, just as they had done three days before. But this time their behavior was peculiar. The men spoke rapidly in high-pitched voices. Some slapped their hands hard against the back of their necks.

"Watch out!" Les muttered. "That means they're mad."

It was very hot as we stood there in the sun. I could feel rivulets of sweat pouring down my face.

What was wrong? Why had they burned the house? We talked together in a low voice, wondering what to do. Les suggested that we give them the presents. Perhaps that would quiet them. Les offered the hunk of meat. The rest of us offered our milk and sugar. They took the meat, the condensed milk, and the sugar. Then they threw everything on the ground. They continued to jabber in their high tone. I saw they were really angry about something. I thought: "This is it." In my mind I said: "Lord, make death quick if it must come."

The Indian women came forward once more to whine, protest, and assail us with words. Again they were in a rage. This time three of the men also stalked up to us. They held the points of their arrows to our chests and, in sign language, delivered an unmistakable message: We had better do what the women wanted—or else. Pointing to the barbs on the arrowheads, they showed how it would hurt when we tried to pull these barbs out. (We were well aware of that already!) The women's whines rose to heated shouts. Now they stood with their noses no more than a foot from ours and flailed their arms. One and then another would give us a shove. Who were the more vicious—the men or the women?

Les, who had faced a similar situation before, tried a tactic which had worked then. He walked slowly up to the chief and began stroking his hair. He tugged lightly on the chief's goatee, patted him on the chest, felt his arm muscles admiringly, and generally made a big to-do over him. In soothing tones, he said, "Now chiefy, you're a good boy, when you're asleep. Just calm down—

you might hurt my buddies here. Doesn't that feel good, though, chiefy, having me inflate your ego like this? Now be a good boy and tell your friends to behave."

The chief gazed at Les the way a dog looks up into his master's face. He raised his eyebrows and beamed. He loved this recognition. He calmed down, but the others were edgy and nervous. We knew we were still in trouble. We had to think of something to distract them. Don turned his back and suddenly music filled the air. The Indians were spellbound. They had never heard music before. Then he turned to face them and showed his hands—empty. Again he turned his back; again came the music. He was playing a concealed mouth organ. Going on this way for several minutes, he succeeded in completely puzzling them.

When the concert was over, Toughy decided he wanted my shirt. I had noticed his eying it before and warned my companions to stay close by me. He gave it a few tugs and mumbled something. I shook my head and looked away. He tugged a little harder and began roughing me up a bit. Les led the others in a chorus of protests to the chief. The chief said something to Toughy. He stopped, reluctantly, and slunk away like a spoiled child. Sure enough, it looked as if our tactic was beginning to work.

The atmosphere had completely changed for the better. All seemed relaxed.

"I think we're on pretty good terms with them now," Les said. "Let's get them to talk and try putting some of their words down."

I took from my pocket a pencil and a pad of paper. Toughy was speaking. I started to write down what he said. Suddenly, Witchy began to slap the back of his neck. Then he made a grab, snatched the paper, and tore it up. He seized my pencil and broke that, all the while mumbling something in a high-pitched tone. Then he stood back, still yipping, and glared at me defiantly.

The look in his glazed eyes was eerie and unnerving. This was the first time Witchy had gone into action. Physically smaller than the rest, habitually walking with a crouch, he had so far kept pretty much to himself. But now I could feel his psychic force, as though he were a ready channel for powerful, unseen forces. The others must have felt it, too, for they began to jabber their disapproval of the writing.

"Must be something about it scares him," Les said.

"Maybe he's afraid we're going to give him competition," Don added.

Just then we were startled by a yell from Paul Mason. Roughneck was giving him a bad time over his camera. I looked up in time to see the Indian give Paul's Brownie such a jerk that I wondered his head was still on. Les complained loudly to the chief, who said something to the offender. Roughneck stopped. The chief came up, examined the camera curiously, and wanted to know if there were anything good to eat inside. Roughneck was sulking by himself a few feet away. I could tell he was still smarting from the chief's rebuke, and was just waiting to give vent to his feelings. So I suggested we missionaries take a walk down to the creek a short distance away. Some of us stood on the near bank; others sat on the big log which lay across the creek.

"Paul! Look out!" I cried. "Roughneck has his arrow drawn on you!" I sucked in my breath. The troublemaker, who had been lurking behind us, was standing a few yards shy of the creek, his muscles bulging, slowly pulling the arrow all the way back.

Les yelled to the chief. The rest of us shouted and waved our arms to show our opposition. Paul whirled around and faced Roughneck. "I'll look him straight in the eye," Paul said. "I bet he isn't man enough to shoot me face to face."

We admired Paul's nerve. We were beginning to think he had won his point when *Whoong!* Roughneck had let the arrow go.

It missed Paul's right ear by about three inches. The Yuquis as archers are too expert not to hit a man at that range; it was done intentionally, as if to say, "That was a warning. Don't go giving me a bad time or the next one will get you."

We continued to object, but by now we had had enough threats for one day. "Let's get out of here as quick as we can," I said to

Les. As I saw a clearing ahead, however, another idea struck me. "Hey, Les! Let's try planting some corn, to give them the idea of getting food that way."

"I'm as anxious to get out of here as you are," he said, "but you're right. Let's not give up too quickly. That's a good idea—we'll try it."

As best I could, I explained to the Yuquis that I was going to put some corn in the ground. With my hand, I showed them how high the stalks would be in one moon, then in two, three; and at four moons they would have a lot of corn to eat. Toughy went with me and Roughneck followed Les. We began poking holes in the ground. We put a couple of kernels in each hole, then covered them up. Toughy stood and watched me until he got the idea. Then he waited to put the kernels in while I poked the holes. But Roughneck, as usual, was giving Les trouble. Every time Les poked a hole in the ground and dropped in a couple of kernels, Roughneck made him dig them up again. Les couldn't get any planted at all, but Toughy—who was more agreeable—and I got quite a patch planted.

As hungry as they are, I thought, they ought to be glad to learn how to grow food and should feel friendly toward us for teaching them. Or were they thinking of us only as temporary means toward their ends, after which they would kill us?

Meanwhile, Paul had worked his way to a position from which he could take pictures of us planting. Not daring to put the camera up to his eye, for fear the Indians would think it were a gun, he snapped the pictures from waist level. He reached the end of the roll, then shambled off down to the creek as if to get a drink. There, he unloaded the film and put it in his trouser leg, which was tucked inside his socks, for safekeeping—just in case the Indians eventually took the camera. (As it turned out, this was all fruitless: the camera had not been pointed properly.)

Shortly afterward, the Indians invited us to sit with them around one of their fires, under a palm roof. It was an act of friendship.

But it seemed, as things generally did with the Yuquis, to have a double implication. As we sat there, the atmosphere was like the calm before a storm.

Before long a Yuqui woman began making advances toward one of our fellows. (Les had briefed us earlier that this was not unusual among them. The Yuquis, unlike many primitive tribes, are entirely free and open about sex.) We knew it was very important to avoid showing disgust. On an earlier occasion, when two Yuquis tried to force one of our missionaries to have relations with one of their women, he had made no secret of his disgust. The chief became furious and hit him hard under the chin, giving him a bad cut on the tongue. The only way out of these situations was either to try to divert their attention or to stand up suddenly and walk away as if one had just thought of something.

Les leaped suddenly to his feet, pointed, and held his hand behind his ear. *"Puerco! Puerco!"* he said in hushed tones. We followed his lead and said the same Spanish word for pig, pointing, grunting to imitate the animals, and listening. The Indians, distracted, forgot the advances of the woman.

A few minutes later Toughy and Roughneck began making pig sounds and pointing down a trail. They wanted us to follow them: they would show us how they hunted. We were wary, and sauntered behind them slowly. Some of the others began to prod us from behind. We did not at all like the idea of heading down the trail with those unpredictable two. I stopped a moment and got the chief's attention. With sign language, I indicated that the sun was getting low in the sky, and it was time for us to leave.

However, my plan seemed to interfere with whatever Toughy had in mind for us. He walked up to me and put one hand behind my neck. I could not believe this was the same man who had been placidly planting corn a few moments before. Then he went for my throat. He jammed the thumb and fingers of the other hand deep on either side of my larynx. He squeezed until I was choking desperately. Perhaps he wasn't squeezing as hard as he could, but it was hard enough so that I couldn't breathe. I thought of using the judo

I had learned in the Navy to escape his grip, but restrained myself for a moment in the belief that that might enrage him and we'd be killed.

The pressure built up in my head. My heart seemed to be hammering away in my neck. My lungs wanted to inhale so badly they seemed about to cave in. I began to black out. I said to myself, "Lord, I commend my soul into Your hands."

At that moment Toughy let go. I gasped for breath and slowly recovered my senses. I understood that he had done this to demonstrate his superiority. I did not object at this point! My throat was so sore I could hardly swallow. The other missionaries had been choked, too. The Indians prodded us along. All the others, including the chief, followed.

"I'd like to know what they're up to," I said. "It doesn't look too good."

Les answered, "This is the first time they've forced us like this."

I thought of breaking loose and running—but that might be just the act to incite them to kill; they would probably assume I was running after a gun. There seemed nothing to do but put our fate into their hands, and into His.

When we reached the spot where the first contact was made, Les warmed them up by pointing out that, just as he had given them gifts there before, we would bring some again. Then, thinking they were back in a good mood, Les showed it was time for each of us to head for our respective camps. Fingers closed about my throat and the throats of my companions once more! The choking, though not so hard as before, was just as convincing.

But a few minutes later the chief abruptly announced we could leave. What a relief that was!

We headed for home. Normally, the Yuquis would tag along for about a hundred yards and then, after we had assured them we would return, slip back into the jungle. But this time, for a mile or more, they still followed us. We wondered what was up.

We soon found out: arrows began whizzing over our heads. Startled, we turned to see what they were doing. The Yuquis were laughing; they were just having fun at our expense, to see how close they could come without hitting us.

"These guys sure have a deadly sense of humor," I said solemnly.

When all their arrows were gone, they ran ahead to retrieve them. Then they would fall back and shoot them past us again. Chills ran up and down my back each time I heard the arrows whishing by. I thought: "I hope these guys are as accurate with their misses as they are with their hits." I knew how William Tell's son must have felt when he saw his dad pulling back on the bow. One Indian lost an arrow in the bushes. Although we were still shaking inwardly from the frightening experience, we nevertheless helped him look until we found it. As with the choking, we thought we had better go along with their games—or risk having them aim to kill the next time.

We walked on and they kept behind us—without any more archery practice. But in a few minutes they came up to stop us. By sign language they showed us that many moons ago, long before we had made a friendly contact, they had seen us coming along the trail past this very spot. They had fully intended to kill us then, but waited too long with drawn arrows.

"The Lord had His guardian angels working overtime that day," I said.

"I wonder how many more times they came near killing us?" Les remarked.

We went on. Farther along the trail, they showed us the spot where they had been in hiding when some Bolivian farmers came through. They had shot one. They went through the motions of shooting one arrow and then another. One Indian gave an imitation of the farmer screaming as he fell; others imitated the Bolivians' guns going *boom-boom* and frightening them away.

Finally, they stopped us to say this was as far as they were going. It had been more than three miles. Then what I had been dreading happened. The women began to whine and howl once more. Now it was clear that they were pleading for the return of the four children whom the Bolivians still had in captivity. When we gave them no positive assurance that we could do so, they began shoving us and signaling unmistakably that we had *better* bring them back—or face the consequences. The men's voices rose to a high pitch of excitement; they slapped the back of their necks angrily as they talked. We tried to disclaim any knowledge about the children (it was true we couldn't find two of them). They threatened to wreak their revenge on the farmers if we didn't comply with their demand. We felt sorry for them, but there was nothing we could do. Not getting anywhere, the chief changed his tack; mildly, he asked us to bring some sugar next time we came.

After we parted from them, we spoke very few words—we were too emotionally wrung. Besides, our throats were sore.

We reached the river just before dark. When Les started the outboard motor, it was a comforting sound. I felt glad to be alive, to be protected again by the trappings of civilization. Later that evening, as we sat around the table in the Fosters' house, we agreed to postpone further contacts for a few days. Among other reasons, our nerves, as well as our throats, needed the rest. Also, if we stayed away for awhile, we thought it might show our disapproval of the Yuquis' threats and rough treatment. If they wanted our gifts, they would have to learn to treat us better.

Before we could make contact again I had a letter from Edith, saying the children were due for their two weeks' June vacation. Les and Lois went up to Cochabamba with me to see their children. This time we traveled by banana truck—two days and nights of winding road. On the afternoon we arrived, the phone rang for Les. The radio communications office uptown wanted him to come right over—there was a top priority message from Todos Santos. When Les returned, he said, "It was Bob Wilhelmson. The Yuquis just kidnaped a Bolivian boy. The farmers are really up in arms. He thinks we'd better get back there right away."

14

Desperate Stand at the Stronghouse

"CPL7F, CPL7F, are you on, Les? This is CPM6A calling. Over." I was trying to get through to Les Foster in Todos Santos, the routine daily radio contact we at the Cochabamba headquarters kept with all the outposts.

The radio was crackled with static. I gave Les another call.

"This is CPL7F. How are you reading me this afternoon, Bruce? Over."

"You're coming in fine. Over."

"I'm glad of the chance to talk to you," Les said. "Oh, pray for us, Bruce. I just heard that the farmers are planning to go to La Jota. They're going to put some poisoned sugar in the place where we've been leaving our gifts. Over."

I caught my breath. "That's terrible!" I said. "Isn't there anything you can do to stop them? Over."

"That isn't even the worst," Les went on. "The farmers have put it up to us to get their kidnaped boy back. They give us a month. Then, if we don't deliver, they're going into the jungle and wipe out the Yuquis. Even if it means sacrificing the life of the boy. Did you get me on that? Over."

My hands were wet as I gripped the microphone. "Be very, very careful, Les. Think twice before you try making another contact. Over."

That's just what we were thinking, Bruce. But we've got to go out to La Jota every night to make sure the farmers don't leave that poisoned sugar. Over."

"I'm going up to La Paz again, Les, to see if I can persuade the government to give some financial help to those farmers. But I'll be back soon. Remember, any time you need me, just holler. If you have nothing more I'll be off and clear."

I turned away from the radio; my heart was in a turmoil. I pitied the farmers their poverty and daily dangers. I could understand their instinct to defend themselves. I pitied the Yuquis, too: the loss of their children would tear the heart out of any human being. At the same time I felt a renewed bitterness at the farmers for trying to poison the Yuquis, and a new resentment at the Indians for their mean and deceitful behavior. But I knew I had to overcome these feelings before I could think and plan clearly. "Lord," I prayed, "give me a new love for both the Indians and the farmers. This resentment and bitterness must go, for if I harbor these emotions, they will lead me to think and do that which is not pleasing to You."

Previously, when for several weeks no Indians had appeared, Les had decided to take advantage of their absence to construct an impregnable base of operations. First he had had an airstrip built about two miles southeast of La Jota near where we had made the contacts. To one side of the airstrip he had built a kind of fortified house, a house in which we could easily be protected in case of attack. A radio transmitter and a generating plant were included, so that it would be possible to keep in touch with the outside world from there. By the time the Yuquis returned, Les had had his stronghouse ready.

In Cochabamba, I was enjoying a bright Sunday afternoon at the missionary home. It was December, 1959. For once it was quiet in the yard. The children were either taking their naps or walking with their mothers.

My mind was very much on my friends out there on that lonely airstrip deep in the jungle. When four-thirty came, I gave Les a call.

With no explanation, he plunged right in. "Bruce, can you get down here quick to give us a hand? Over." The quaver in his voice told me the situation was serious.

"I'll see what I can do," I said. "Can you tell me what's wrong? Over."

"A bunch of Yuquis just left here. I'm sure thankful we have this radio. I don't know how I'd get word out otherwise . . . Boy, they sure roughed us up this time. They gave us real trouble. I don't know what got into them . . ."

For a couple of minutes Les couldn't talk. He was choked full of emotion. I had never seen him weep, but over the radio I heard him.

He began again. "I don't want to break off the contact unless it seems hopeless. Can you come down, Bruce, and bring another man? Over."

"I'll let you know in five minutes, Les," I answered.

While another missionary was using the radio, I went outside to think things over. It was a very difficult time for me to help him out. I was supposed to leave in a couple of days to go assist in the reopening of the school for missionary children in Tambo, seven hours' bus ride from Cochabamba in the foothills. They were counting on me there to do administrative work, bookkeeping, and some teaching. There was a great deal to be taken care of before school started in a few weeks.

I weighed things. On Les's side, it was a matter of life and death. No need at the school could be greater than that. I decided to go to Todos Santos. But I would try not to stay away for more than two weeks at the most.

I went back into the radio room. "This is CPM6A, Les," I called, "there's a plane to Todos Santos tomorrow. I'll try and get on it.

I'll see if I can get another fellow or two. I'll wait until dark to head out, so meet me along the trail somewhere. Over." (I didn't want to go during the day with a couple of new men, for it would be very dangerous.) Les was overjoyed to hear I was coming.

All the rooms of the mission compound opened onto a patio. I went around to the one occupied by Chuck Johnson and his family, and knocked. Chuck's huge frame filled the doorway. He had the shoulders of a wrestler and hands like hams. "This is my man," I thought to myself.

A Canadian, Chuck had been a male nurse in a mental hospital. He had often described to me how he would keep unruly patients under control with his authoritative stare—or, that failing, subdue them physically. He was a human dynamo. After he joined our mission, he would work hard all day, then drive hours to address a meeting in some little town and be back at work the next morning. He'd been through a tough bootcamp training in the mountains of British Columbia.

"What's up, friend?" he asked.

"I just talked to Les Foster on the radio."

"So? Come on in and have a cup of coffee."

"Thanks, Chuck. But there's no time for coffee now. He's in real trouble. He wants me to come down right away and bring a couple of fellows with me. I wondered if—"

"That's for me, boy!" Chuck interrupted. "When do we start?"

Through the open doorway I glimpsed a peaceful family scene: Chuck's wife and his four children were sitting around a table practicing their Spanish on one another. I had qualms.

"Chuck," I said in a low voice so as not to alarm his family, "I feel you should know exactly what I'm letting you in for. Les is in contact with the Yuquis. They're mean, tough, and unpredictable. You're likely to get choked or poked with arrows. There's even a fair chance we could get killed. Nothing says you have to go, you know."

He laughed. "Isn't that what I came down here for? The last nine months I've had my nose in a Spanish book. And the Indians we want to reach don't even speak Spanish! I'm bursting for action. Do you think I'm going to pass up a chance like this? Now tell me what to take."

We talked about who else might go. Chuck suggested Hudson Birkett, and we went around to his room. Hudson was British. Like Chuck, he, too, had been a male nurse. But he didn't fit the part. Slender, fair, and soft-spoken, Hudson looked more like a scholar. I had misgivings about him, for he had come straight to the field from Manchester with his wife, Joan, and missed the ardors of bootcamp training. But his eagerness was equal to Chuck's.

"I'd love to have a go at it, if you don't mind," he said with his quiet smile. When I told him, as I had told Chuck, of what lay ahead, he remained unruffled. "I'll start getting my gear together."

The three of us made out our lists of essential supplies.

The next morning we were at the airport at the crack of dawn. Among the well-dressed people heading for La Paz we looked like commandos, with our packsacks, heavy work shoes, neatly pressed tan trousers, and shirts. Chuck and Hudson were fairly bursting with excitement.

As the two-motored plane gunned its engines on the end of the runway, I wondered if I would see Cochabamba again, if I would press my lips again to Edith's as we said good-by. She took it as calmly as ever, for she had the confidence the Lord would protect me as He had on other occasions.

Lois Foster was at the airstrip in Todos Santos to meet us. She looked very worried. At her house, she prepared dinner while we made arrangements with a Bolivian to ferry us upriver. In case there might be trouble with the outboard motor, we started shortly after midday. There was no trouble, however, and we reached the abandoned farmhouse about twilight.

"Let's relax," I said. "We'd better wait here until dark so we won't run across the Indians along the trail." But Chuck, too excited to sit down, paced back and forth.

The farm was overgrown with heavy underbrush. Its occupants had fled long ago. The air was heavy. Thick clouds rolled in from the west, and the sun disappeared prematurely. It was dusk.

"Okay, fellows," I said as I got up to put on my heavy pack. "It's dark enough to go. I'm sure the Indians are off the trail by now. I wouldn't be surprised if we get wet before we get there." Hudson and Chuck dug out their flashlights and loaded on their packs, one helping the other.

Under the canopy of jungle trees it was pitch black. As usual, the trail was muddy. It was very difficult to balance on the slippery, mossy logs. The heavy clouds seemed to be pressing down hard upon us.

In La Jota, Les was waiting for us. "Thank heaven you've come!" he said. We hugged each other. He went on, "I figured you'd be along about ten o'clock, but I came out early just in case."

We kept on another hour, slogging through cold slippery mud. A light rain was falling. Our flashlights hardly made dents in the darkness. When we reached camp, we took a cold dip in the creek, and how wonderful it felt to get into dry clothes. A fire was burning under the palm-thatched roof of the shack beside the airstrip. Dick and Harold put some more wood on it. Les pointed out the stronghouse about fifty yards away—it was barely visible in the dark— then began telling us what had happened.

"Yesterday the Yuquis showed up across the stream. They had the kidnaped Bolivian boy with them."

"It was the first time we knew he was alive," Dick said. "He looked to be in good shape."

"We tried to get them to bring him over," Les continued, "but they wouldn't."

I sat looking at the fire, thinking. "How did they act?" I asked.

"Pretty mean, I would judge," Les said somberly.

"I wonder," I said, half to myself, "if they're beginning to give up hope that they can use us to get their children back?"

"Maybe so."

"If that's the case, they have probably concluded they might as well get rid of us. We'd better keep that possibility uppermost in our minds if we think about making another contact."

We continued to talk for an hour or so. The rain was pouring down hard. Lightning lit up all the surrounding jungle, with the thunder tumbling after. About midnight we slung our hammocks under the palm-thatched roof and crawled in.

The dawn was gray and wet. This, we knew, would keep the Yuquis away. Les took us over to inspect the stronghouse. My first good look at it was reassuring. It somewhat reminded me of an old-style gas station at home, the kind that had the roof hanging over the pumps. But it was strong and solid. Two rows of flattened gasoline drums had been nailed against the outside, making a crude wall of armor plate about seven feet high. This left a crack under the roof, through which the light could filter.

The second floor was built like a tent, with room enough to stand up in the middle, but sloping at the sides with the pitch of the roof right down to the eaves. The roof was covered with sheets of aluminum, in case the Yuquis tried to shoot fire arrows to burn us out.

Les had put a big combination padlock on the front door. "I want you all to work the combination right now until you know it by heart," he said. "This is necessary so we can all get in quickly in case of a surprise attack." We spent the rest of the morning on that assignment.

Early the second day, a long, low, mournful whistle came across the stream. "Get all the clothes off the line and lock them up inside!" Les shouted. "The Yuquis will show up at any minute."

He went out on the big log that crossed the creek in back of the stronghouse. He moved slowly toward the riverbank. Holding up his hands, he returned the whistle. No Yuqui appeared. He waved his arms, motioning to them to come on over. Two or three showed themselves, then others. They were still hesitant. Les held up some cans of sugar which he had kept outside. Some of us were still in the stronghouse.

"Better all come out in the open where they can see you!" Les called. We did. More and more heads poked out from behind the trees to look us over. Cautiously, they picked their way over the log. We could see their heads turn this way and that. Their black eyes, on the alert for surprises, darted in all directions.

"The ones just coming over now we call Roughneck and Toughy," I explained to Hudson.

He was staring open-mouthed. "I should say those chaps are well named," he observed mildly. "I've never seen more grisly characters in my life."

When they were all across the river, they moved forward to join us in the clearing beside the airstrip. Les counted them. "Evidently the farmers didn't put the sugar out," he said. "I don't see any Indians missing."

That eased our nervousness somewhat. For the first hour or so our visitors were in a good mood. They tried several times to pull out our eyebrows and eyelashes; but when Les complained to the chief, they desisted. Perhaps they were only hoping to make us look more like themselves.

"I'm glad I shaved my chest," grinned Chuck.

"This isn't as bad as I had imagined," said Hudson.

Then, the strange actions of Witchy caught my attention. He seemed to be carrying on a violent conversation with an unseen person. Every now and then he would pause and slap himself hard on the back of the neck. After Witchy got his orders from the spirit world, he turned around and said something to the others. Roughneck and Toughy walked over to where Hudson and Chuck were standing and, without any warning and for no discernible reason, began choking them. It was not pleasant to watch. As the Indians tightened their grip, I could see the veins pop out on their foreheads. The rest of us objected vigorously. This made the Yuquis all the angrier. Then the chief slapped his own neck and spoke to the Indians. Roughneck and Toughy released their grip.

"You two have just been officially initiated into the chokers' club," I said.

"I didn't actually care to qualify," Hudson remarked, rubbing his neck. The contact went along better after that. We often wondered why the Yuquis were so much meaner on some days than on others. Perhaps, as appeared to have happened just now, it was because the witchdoctor had invoked the demons. About midafternoon they left.

After supper was over, and each one had washed his dish, cup, and spoon, came time for discussion. It was a starry night. A few mosquitoes were buzzing around. We built up the fire, feeding it with the ends of three good-sized logs. New thoughts were in my mind that day, but I waited until this moment to express them.

"You know, fellows," I began, "our stronghouse is no use when we're all outside with the Indians. If they made up their minds all of a sudden to kill us, we wouldn't have time to unlock that combination lock and get inside. They'd plug us full of arrows in a minute. My idea is to keep one man inside from now on. As the last resort, if it looks serious, the man inside could start up the generator to scare them away. If things look as if they are getting ready to kill us, then the fellow inside can shoot the shotgun up in the air. That will enable everyone to get inside the stronghouse until we can get the plane in to haul us out of here."

Everyone regarded this as a sensible and practicable idea. Les cautioned, "We have to make perfectly sure they mean to kill us before we shoot, because once we do, that will be the end of the work."

"That's for sure," Harold added.

"I'd hate to see this contact end up the way the Nhambiguara tribe contact did," I said.

Les began, "I just don't understand why we haven't made progress. We've tried everything I know. We just don't have any more ideas as to how to calm them down and still be friendly. The only thing I can think of is that they're still furious at us for not returning their children."

Everyone fell silent, preoccupied with his own thoughts.

The next morning, as we were eating breakfast, I noticed I was slightly dizzy and feverish. I told the others I must be coming down with the flu.

"That settles it," said Les. "You're elected to be the one who stays inside the stronghouse today. You told me yourself how deadly the flu can be to these primitive people, and it wouldn't be fair to expose the Yuquis. Besides, this would give you the chance you've been waiting for to take your pictures."

I could only agree. When I had finished eating, I climbed the ladder to the second floor. I nailed some cloth over the back wall—on the side toward the creek—so the Indians wouldn't be able to see me through the cracks. Then I loaded the camera. Harold and Dick were out on the airstrip cutting down weeds; the others were reading. The morning was fine; the sun had dried the heavy dew that had dripped from the trees.

Across the creek the whistling began. I rushed upstairs to make sure all the cracks were covered. Already it was stifling under the aluminum roof. I put a shell in the single-barreled shotgun and kept some others handy, just in case. Then I got out my .22 pistol. (We'd had experiences in which the shotgun shells didn't go off because of the dampness.)

The fellows hurried in with their tools because the Indians would help themselves if they were left outside. There was the scramble of taking off watches and emptying pockets while Les went out to whistle back. I lay down on the floor on my belly. Now, I thought, if I can just keep from coughing or sneezing. I didn't want the Yuquis to know I was inside.

Les and the four others took up their positions in the yard behind the stronghouse where the Indians could see them. They were well within range of my camera. Les went over to the creek, got up on the log, and kept on whistling as he motioned the Yuquis to come on over. No one appeared. Les kept on. "Something's wrong," Les said. "They're scared for some reason."

"This is the first time they've hesitated that long," Bob added.

Inside I began to feel uneasy. The Yuquis stayed crouched for nearly fifteen minutes, peering at us. Then the chief poked his head out. He started jabbering something as if asking many questions.

"Put your hands in the air," Les called. "The chief may be wondering if we intend to do them any harm." All arms went up.

The chief strained some more, looking around.

After much persuasion he came out hesitantly. He paused on the log, his eyes fixed on the stronghouse. He carried his bow and arrows, but his arms were crossed in front of his chest. (We had learned by sign language this meant he was afraid. He was protecting his chest from arrows or bullets.) Why, all of a sudden, did he suspect us of wanting to shoot him?

Roughneck, then Toughy, followed slowly, both with their arms in the same position. Then came Witchy, then the others. They were more nervous than I had ever seen them before. Something was radically wrong. Were they planning to kill? I wanted to warn the others of my skepticism, but I didn't dare give away my hiding place. Each one carried his seven-foot bow and several arrows in his left hand.

My heart pounded so hard I could barely hold the camera still as I clicked one picture after another. That clicking sounded in my ears five times as loud as it was. I didn't see how they could help but hear it. The tension and heat under the aluminum roof were making me sweat. I wanted so much to get good pictures; this might be our last opportunity.

The Yuqui women were still in hiding. Les pointed to them and asked the chief in sign language why they didn't come out. This was odd, too, because they had always come out before. Again the chief raised his arms in a crossed position. He was trying to tell Les that the women were frightened, too. To me it was a sure indication that the Yuquis were up to no good. It might well be they didn't want their women around when they gave the signal to kill. They may have felt we might have guns hidden nearby.

The chief noticed my absence. He asked Les if I were upriver fishing. Les diverted him as to my whereabouts.

As had been previously agreed, the fellows were staying close together behind the stronghouse. I checked again to make sure that my guns were within reach. I felt reassured now that my comrades were close enough so that I could keep my eye on them. In a matter of seconds the Yuquis—there were ten or twelve of them now—could draw their arrows and shoot. I would have to grab the gun and shoot in the air before they could let go of their arrows to kill. I felt the tremendous weight of holding the responsibility for five lives in my hands. One cough, one sneeze, would startle the Indians—and who knows what they would do?

Then I saw Toughy looking straight up at me. He must have heard the click of my camera. Les recognized the situation and called out to distract him.

"That was a close one, Bruce," Les said in an even voice, looking in another direction. (Of course the Yuqui didn't know he was talking to me.) "Don't take any more pictures as long as it's quiet."

The savages began to ask what was inside the stronghouse. They always thought we had a "big bird" (the helicopter) inside our cabin. They asked Les to open the door so they could see it. As the flattened barrels we had nailed to the side were high enough so they could not see over the top, one Indian climbed onto the shoulders of another to peek in the cracks just above the metal. Harold and Les began tickling them to distract them. To pull them away would have been to invite a fight. The Indians asked if the "big bird" were sleeping inside. In sign language, Les indicated the "big bird" was a long distance away now, after visiting the day before. He tried to indicate that we had a motor inside which sounded like the helicopter. Several started humming in imitation of the motor's noise.

They had no doubt heard the light plant generator many times, for they had frequently come out of the jungle just as radio communications were ending and the motor was shut off. They could only surmise that the motor was another sort of bird which roared when it flew. We indicated they were not to be allowed inside, lest they harm it.

"Okay, Bruce," Les said, "get your camera ready. I'm going to get Joven to pull back on his bow to shoot into the air for you." Joven did and it was a perfect pose.

Now one woman appeared and approached cautiously. It was the chief's wife. She looked tough and ferocious enough to hold her own in any situation. The others stayed half-hidden on the other side of the creek.

Witchy was off by himself again, talking animatedly to someone who wasn't there. The rest stood close to one another, facing our five men. The chief began describing how, a day or so before, they had killed a couple of Bolivians. Roughneck and Toughy enacted every detail of it. Each time they shot an imaginary arrow, they would suck in air to make a hissing sound. Then came the sound of an arrow hitting flesh. They were expressing pride in their ability to shoot arrows into an enemy before he could fire a gun in self-defense.

I could see the Yuquis were trying to get our five men to go down to the creek with them. The men hesitated. They tried to get the Indians interested in doing other things. But the Indians were overbearing.

"We'd better go along," Les said. "They may want us only to get some fish for them. Anyway, we don't want to anger them. We'll be back as soon as we can, Bruce."

The men walked slowly down the path to the creek. Their voices, coming to me through about one hundred and fifty feet of jungle, were muffled. I could still see Roughneck and Witchy. They stood in the path about halfway between the men and the stronghouse. They kept looking up toward the stronghouse and then glancing down the path. Just the looks of Witchy gave me the creeps. His glassy, elusive eyes indicated he was probably in a trance. When he talked to an unseen person and slapped the back of his neck, I wondered how much he had to do with giving destructive orders to the chief and others. Did his contact with spirits give him more power and authority than the chief? Now both Roughneck and Witchy were slapping their necks. They kept whispering and looking toward me.

They must be planning something. I began to feel the veins in my forehead throb with every heartbeat. They were aware that we didn't know their language; yet, mysteriously, they didn't want to speak loud. They started walking toward me. My first thought was that they would try to break in while the other Indians held the five men down by the river. Time was short. If they started tearing away part of the roof or some boards to get in, they would see me and might kill me. Fear for my life began to tingle through my veins. I had a minute or two to make a decision. Should I hurry down to the ground floor and start the motor? Should I?

No, I thought, it might cause the Yuquis to panic and start killing. I checked again to make sure of the exact position of the guns. The two were right beside me. I pulled back the hammer on the shotgun. Now they were just below me, about three feet away. They were whispering. Oh, what wouldn't I give to know what they were saying! Maybe they were afraid to wake up the "big bird." Roughneck stepped up on the log to peek over the metal wall. He poked his arrow through the cracks, trying to hook onto some of the clothing we had hung on a line inside. It was too dark in there for them to see anything else. Still sick with the flu, I was drenched with sweat from the fever and the heat under the roof. Suddenly I felt I had to cough. The sweat trickled around my ears and off my chin as I swallowed and swallowed to fight down the cough. The sweat tickled and I wanted to scratch, yet I didn't dare move.

Oh, no, I thought. Roughneck was climbing on the shoulders of Witchy to look in on the second floor right where I was lying. Should I scare them away right now by yelling, or by scraping my hands along the corrugated aluminum? That black bushy head was rising just six inches from mine. My heart and breathing seemed to stop. How I wished the men were outside to divert these two! Then Roughneck saw the camera. With a quick motion he poked his finger at it and knocked it over. It fell with a thud. Now I *had* to do something, for the next thing he would do was to peek through the hole and see me. Immediately an idea flashed into my mind. I let out a long, loud groan. It terrified even me.

Whether they thought the "big bird" inside was waking up and would soon start roaring, or what, I don't know. Roughneck jumped down and the two ran off down the path to where they were standing before, halfway between the others and the stronghouse. They looked terrified. What a mystery it must have been to them! With a sigh, I shifted positions and let out a muffled cough. I felt better.

Now my concern shifted back to the men. What was happening to them? The jabbering through the trees sounded normal. If only I could see them!

"BR-U-U-U-CE!" It was a desperate cry from Les. *"Get the gun ready!"* The words hit me like a thunderclap. "Oh, no, Lord," I thought to myself, "has it come to this?" Nervously, I grabbed the shotgun and checked to make sure the shell was inside. The hammer was already pulled back. I sat straining for another word. Perspiration dripped off my nose. I knew Les was usually calm and very careful about making any decision he might later regret; therefore, when he had yelled, I knew the situation was critical. An almost unbearable weight of responsibility was on me. I wondered, are the men being choked? If they are, then I wouldn't be able to get the next command to shoot. If I waited, maybe they would all be choked to death! Should I go ahead and shoot anyway? I pleaded the protection of Jesus Christ that comes in His Name and through His Blood. Yet, I realized God had given me common sense to use, too, in such crises as this. One question pressed in on me: *Should I Shoot?*

In case the shotgun shell had gone bad, I had my pistol ready. The debate went on in my mind for what seemed hours, although it couldn't have been more than four or five minutes. With the pressure to act mounting, I found it hard to concentrate on the talking going on down by the creek. Yet I had to. Timing was everything. If I fired at the right moment I could save the fellows' lives. But firing at the wrong moment could provoke the Yuquis to kill.

I heard Les shout, "They all have their arrows drawn on us." I raised the shotgun and held it; the gun was heavy in my perspiring hands. A minute later Les said, "I'm starting to walk away from them."

"What nerve!" I thought to myself. Then, "He shouldn't do

that." To turn his back would surely be to invite a storm of arrows. My finger on the trigger, I waited. I heard nothing, saw nothing.

I heard Les call out, "Don't shoot, Bruce!"

Another few minutes of silence. Then my friends appeared. They were walking slowly, the Yuquis following. I laid the shotgun down. They gathered in the clearing below me, where I could see them plainly. I shifted my position in case Roughneck and Toughy climbed up again to peek in the hole where the camera had been, and wiped my forehead. I felt like a wet mop.

All seemed calm. Les was standing there, with his arms folded; Chuck and Hudson were seated on a log. Suddenly, without warning, Roughneck and Toughy approached them, bent them over backwards, and choked them. There was a viciousness in their action this time that I had never seen before. They weren't just choking to demonstrate their superiority—they were choking to kill! I got my pistol ready and slipped the safety catch. There were nine shots in it. But I hoped one shot would be enough to frighten them off—short-barreled, my pistol makes a tremendous racket.

Les walked rapidly up to the chief and spoke with a new note of authority in his voice—an authority I saw he had won through his courageous act of turning his back on the drawn arrows.

The chief barked an order. Roughneck and Toughy let go of Chuck and Hudson, who slumped forward, gasping for breath. Roughneck, Toughy, and Witchy—who was lurking a few feet away—glared at the men and slapped their necks in frustrated rage. The chief barked again and walked away. They slunk away after him toward the jungle. Our policy of gaining the upper hand with one small, calculated act after another had paid off.

Then, with deliberate step, almost sauntering, the missionaries moved out of my line of vision. I heard someone—probably Les—working the combination lock. A minute later they were all safe inside the stronghouse. I could barely make it down the ladder, so exhausted was I from sickness, heat, and tension. Chuck and Hudson were still panting, but they weren't seriously hurt.

"Wow!" I said. "What a day!"

Hudson shook his head and added hoarsely, "When they pulled their arrows on us, I thought we were goners!"

"It was agony for me up there, not being able to see you guys," I said. "Still, I can imagine how much worse it must have been for you."

Les then described to me what had happened:

After the Yuquis had lured the missionaries down by the stream, they drew their arrows. Then Les deliberately turned his back on them and walked away. He thought they wouldn't consider it sporting to shoot a man in the back. (Or, we wondered, was he expecting them to react according to our own code, which had no meaning for them?)

Les had gone but a few steps when he couldn't resist glancing back over his shoulder. He looked just in time to see Toughy let his arrow go toward Hudson, then stop it just as the feathers reached his fingers. That was when he had yelled to me to get the gun ready.

We all sat around in a state of collapse, trying to appraise the situation; but in fact everyone was too worked up to do any serious thinking. In a little while Dick prepared supper while the rest of us, trembling now, took baths in the creek.

A bit more relaxed after supper, we lingered around the fire. We tried to figure out how the Yuquis felt.

"I bet those guys are smarting yet," I began. "This is without a doubt the first time anyone has stood up to them without getting shot in return. It may be to our advantage—or it may just be that this is so frustrating to them that the next time they'll really vent their wrath on us. The powers of darkness from which Witchy gets his orders start all the trouble. When he left with the others I sure didn't like those last looks he gave us. It may be they are coming to the conclusion that it is best to polish us off. We're really on very, very dangerous ground."

"What do you think, Bruce, of our chances of maintaining a friendly contact?" Les asked.

I hardly knew what to say. But I tried. "It's evident things are getting progressively worse. We've given the Yuquis every possible chance to be friendly and gain confidence in us. I don't know of one thing we've done to provoke them to kill us, unless it was the fact that we didn't bring back their four children. Even there, we did everything we could. I don't know, it seems if we haven't gotten anywhere in twenty-two tries we probably never will. Yet we mustn't forget that these people have souls, and if we pull out it will mean they will probably never have another chance to hear the story of salvation. Still, if we continue, we may not live to tell someone else about the Gospel."

Les added, "We must remember this: the minute we leave, the farmers will declare all-out war against the Yuquis. The Indians are our responsibility."

"Let's spend some time in prayer," Dick said. "What counts is that we all have peace in our hearts, whether we continue or pull out." Our main concern as we prayed was, first, that we might be faithful to His will, even unto death. Verses of Scripture came to my mind: "Looking unto Jesus the author and finisher of our faith; who for the joy that was set before him endured the cross, despising the shame, and is set down at the right hand of the throne of God. For consider him that endured such contradiction of sinners against himself, lest ye be wearied and faint in your minds. Ye have not yet resisted unto blood, striving against sin" (Heb. 12:2-4).

The time of prayer over, Les gave his opinion. "My thought is that we continue the contact. We'll keep one man inside, for I think that's an excellent precaution. If the Yuquis draw blood, then we'll pull out." Everyone concurred. If we had to pull out we wanted to do it in such a way that months later we could attempt another contact, should we feel His leading.

For nearly two weeks the Yuquis didn't show up. They had shot two more nationals, and, no doubt fearing the farmers' fury, probably left the area. It was imperative that I return to Cochabamba to take up my neglected work at our school. I didn't like leaving the fellows, but they urged me to go ahead, for they understood my pressing duty. And the safety factor of the one man inside the stronghouse gave me some reassurance. So, with a few qualms, I bade the others farewell and went back to Cochabamba.

A few days later, I was walking into the room of the missionary house where the radio was and happened to glance out the window. Chuck and Hudson were marching toward me across the yard. When I ran out to meet them, I noticed Chuck's hand was bandaged.

"What happened?" I asked anxiously.

Chuck began. "I got an arrow in my hand. We had to pull out of the contact."

"How in the world did it happen?"

"Well, the day after Christmas the Yuquis came out again. We spent a few hours fooling around—fishing, racing, and so on. In sign language, they motioned for Les to call for the 'big bird' to come and sit down on the landing strip. We knew Jonathan Tamplin of the World Gospel Mission was due any minute, for we had made arrangements for him to bring in supplies. We thought it would be fun to see their surprise when the plane came. In the meantime, Toughy showed off his strength to the rest of us by shooting his arrows nearly out of sight. While pulling back hard on one of those long arrows, he snapped his bow in two. It was really funny, but no one dared laugh. He was thoroughly disgusted. Just then the plane was heard, and the Yuquis took off like scared rabbits. Lois Foster and Joan Birkett came along with some supplies. Les went out to warn Jonathan that the Indians were around and not to shut off the motor. The women stepped out and we helped unload the supplies. Lois handed us a delicious cherry pie! The women were going to stay a few hours, while Jonathan planned on making more flights with supplies from Todos Santos; but Les told the women they'd better go back right away.

"We hurried and ate some pie while the plane motor was still going. Just after Jonathan took off, the Yuquis came back out. They saw the crumbs around our mouths and became angry—I suppose because we didn't give them any. There was none left.

Toughy began to poke me with his arrow—remember, he had broken his bow. Then he stepped back and threw a couple of arrows hard, like spears. I dodged them both. The third arrow came so fast that I had no time to move. I guess my reflex action caused me to raise my hands to my chest. Just as I did his arrow went into my hand quite a ways. If it hadn't gone into my hand, it would have gone right into my heart and I wouldn't be here today. Les yelled for Harold to start the generator inside the stronghouse. He got it going and it scared them away. I stopped the bleeding as best I could with pressure on my wrist. Then Les went in and got his pistol and turned the motor off. The Indians began whistling. Les walked toward them a little ways. He held his pistol straight up, pointed to my bloody hand, and said 'No! No! No!' The Yuquis seemed to understand that Les meant business, for they all melted away.

"Jonathan made eight more trips, and flew us and all of our things out. Believe me, it was a heartache to make the decision that afternoon in the stronghouse to pull out of the contact."

"What are Les's plans now?" I asked Chuck.

"That man isn't giving up," Chuck replied. "He's going to spend some time thinking and praying about it and try again at another time and in another way."

15

Regrouping for Victory

Three years have passed since we broke off contact with the Yuquis.

But neither those nor the preceding three, in which we made twenty-four contacts, have been wasted. Looking back over six years in perspective—they gave us the needed groundwork for the larger undertaking yet to come.

In 1963, as I write this, we are getting ready to try again. Les Foster and Dick Strickler, after their year's furlough in the States, are now back in the front lines at Todos Santos. Two other missionaries and their families have gone there to help them lay the foundations for the campaign ahead. As soon as other assignments permit, I hope to join them.

We face the greatest challenge of our missionary careers—an effort that will almost certainly take more of our time and energy and will involve us in greater risks than any we have ever attempted.

We will go armored not only with our belief that the Lord will watch over us, but with our hard-won knowledge gained by our combined experiences over the years. We go fully mindful of the dangers and obstacles that lie like a minefield in wait for us—but we go prepared to deal with them.

Our target is still the Yuquis, whom we yet hope to reach with the Gospel.

Since our contacts ended, we have learned from oil explorers that the Yuquis whom we met on the trail were only one small group. Nevertheless, it was only through dealing with them that we were able to become familiar with their dangerous deceitfulness, their complex psychology, their pattern of living, and the threats that haunt their lives.

This time we hope to reach the main cluster of the Yuqui tribe, believed to be still living in their heartland, which is only forty or fifty miles from Todos Santos as the crow flies. But to find them we will have to travel a distance of one hundred and fifty miles down the Rio Chaparé, and two hundred miles up the Rio Ichilo, along two sides of a long narrow triangle.

The area which the Yuquis inhabit and which we must traverse for many days to reach them, remains one of the most mysterious and little-known parts of the earth.

We have learned from the few who have ventured into this forbidding terrain that here is a land of towering jungle trees and great dank ferns; a land of sudden torrential downpours, flooding the rivers and alternating with periods of parching drought; a region rife with strange poisonous plants and vines, with many kinds of deadly snakes, with scorpions whose sting may mean death, with tarantulas measuring twelve inches across that can spring two feet in one leap. Here also we expect to find other aboriginal tribes besides the Yuquis—tribes concerning whose deadly savagery we can only speculate.

Over the past three years, in personal conference or by letter, we have been laying our plans. They are now almost complete. Our overall strategy is based on what we know to be the most plaguing problem of the Yuquis—hunger.

When their homeland is washed out by floods, the groups scatter into other areas, seizing their food where they can find it and preying on the farms of the already deprived Bolivians. So our strategy is to start a farm on high ground in the midst of Yuqui territory—a Utopia to them, a place where they could help themselves without being accused of stealing. In this way we hope to bring to fruition the crude experiment started almost by accident that day on the Yuqui trail in La Jota, when I showed Toughy how to plant corn.

To minimize our dangers, Les is having a veritable floating stronghouse built. This unique craft—bargelike, flat-bottomed, and snub-nosed—is an adaptation of the mail boats on which we traveled the Guaporé. It incorporates many of the protective features Les built into our La Jota stronghouse. Because of its wide, flat bottom, the boat will be able to carry a heavy load yet draw only a few inches of water, making for easy maneuvering over sandbars and sunken logs. The living quarters will have sturdy walls, like the siding of a house, and heavy wooden doors. Even the windows will be equipped with heavy wooden shutters. Both windows and doors will have heavy locks, so that no hostile tribesmen can force their way in. The afterdeck, where the diesel engine is located, will be protected by a heavy mesh screen. A radio transmitter and receiver will enable the missionary crew to keep in contact with headquarters in Todos Santos and to summon help in case of emergency. Our floating stronghouse will carry six months' provisions.

Many days of preparation have gone into this expedition, and many more will follow. No purpose other than taking the story of salvation to the Indians, changing their age-old ways, and stopping their endless wars would be worth the effort.

Yes, the physical barriers to our renewed assault will be great, and wise tactics and strong armor are required to surmount them. Yet our greatest barriers, just as in the past, will continue to come from within ourselves. No physical stronghouse or strategy will defeat the enemies within. Only experience, courage, and, above all, faith, will help us there.

Experience has taught me something of what to expect on the

"inner battlefield." One persistent enemy is fear—and it comes in many guises. There is, for example, fear of loss of support at home, fear that if so-and-so-many souls are not reported saved, funds will be cut and a long-term effort frustrated. I am sorry to say that this has happened in some cases. Yet the pioneer missionary, pouring out his heart and life to reach tribes, need only trust completely in Jesus Christ: for I have found that when I did this, my needs were always met somehow.

There is also the fear of losing one's life. Yes, I know what the Bible says concerning death—that to be absent from the body is to be present with the Lord, which is joy unspeakable. And yet there were many times when I did not have the courage to accept this wholeheartedly, times when the instinct for self-preservation rose before the inner voice like a wall. Many times, too, I was afraid I would do the wrong thing at a time of crisis. To conquer this, I developed the habit of picturing in advance each possible situation, then rehearsing in my mind what action I should take if and when it occurred. Also, I reminded myself of the promise, "In all thy ways acknowledge Him, and He shall direct thy paths."

Beyond the barrier of fear lies the barrier of impatience. I had to learn painfully that missionary time is something different from the time of worldly affairs. Waiting for our supplies that first time in Cochabamba—how endless it seemed! How impatient I was, and how much less so would I be now! Then comes the long task of reaching the Indians at all, and once one does, the frustrating job of trying to overcome all the obstacles within the native soul. To release him from the demons he worships, it is necessary to sit around a campfire with him for months, first listening to find out *why* he believes, finally spending many, many more patient months in giving him the Word of God that will deliver him from the evil spirits and doom.

Many of the Indian' actions try the patience to the breaking point. Our love is sorely tested when, after working painstakingly day after day to learn a tribe's speech, we discover they have deliberately given us the wrong words.

Understanding the native's deep fear of the white man is the first step in overcoming such frustration. As we have seen, in some places "civilized" man had years ago killed off thousands of Indians and kidnaped thousands of women and children, virtually forcing the Indians to shun civilization thereafter. Believing that sooner or later we will do them harm, the Indians study every move we make carefully, so that it is incredibly difficult to win their confidence. Holding out one's arms in a friendly way toward one of their children portrays the same picture to them as enticing the young-sters to come closer in order to snatch them away. A wrong action with pure motives can endanger a missionary's life and do almost irreparable damage to the relationship.

Impatience and frustration can lead directly to what can become the missionary's greatest single enemy: depression. This is a weapon that strikes without warning, and it can be devastating. Alone or nearly alone, ill-fed, exhausted, rebuffed by every force human or inhuman, the missionary is often close to the brink of hopelessness —I myself was, after Dave was killed. Through such experiences, common sense will help, but only the power of God and His love within will enable one to pull himself together and go on.

As I look back over my years of difficult life on the trail, of weeks spent away from my family, of frustrations, disappointments, and defeats, I sometimes ask myself, "And what do I have to show for it all?" To give an honest account of my stewardship, I must answer: "In the way of tangible evidence of tribes which I have reached personally with the Gospel, of primitive people living ac-cording to God's plan and desire as the result of my own efforts—very little."

But I am in no way disheartened or discouraged. We know this is the lot of the pioneer missionary. Ours is the difficult role of making first contacts. We are the advance soldiers in the vanguard of the Lord, Commandos for Christ. It is for us to furrow the ground. It is for others to plant the seed and reap the harvest.

And as surely as day follows night, the harvest will come. And it will be rich, the result of all the hard plowing, sowing, and watering that has been done, in tears, heartaches, suffering, and blood. Our accounting to God is for faithfulness, not for results.

"Moreover, it is required in stewards, that a man be found faithful" (I Cor. 4:2).

". . . he that ploweth should plow in hope . . ." (I Cor. 9:10).

"One soweth, and another reapeth" (John 4:37).

Our faith is not unsupported. There is unmistakable evidence of our progress. With my own eyes, I have seen tribes at a far more primitive stage of savagery than those I have contacted, reached with the Gospel during the time I have been carrying on my work. With my own eyes, I have seen sworn enemies sitting peaceably together in Bible classes, heathen warriors learning to live by Holy Writ.

I cite as one example to support my faith, my visit to the Ayores. There I have seen former killers gather for worship. It was they, it will be remembered, who killed the five missionaries mentioned in Chapter 2. Since that time, wave after wave of missionaries poured in to reach them. The conditions were incredibly difficult. Some pulled out because of discouragement, others because of ill health. But as fast as the spiritually or physically "wounded" left the field, "shock troops of the Lord" went in to take their places. Problems that seemed insoluble were eventually overcome by faith and determination.

For years, one grim practice of the Ayores eluded all efforts to eradicate it. As he went along a jungle path, a missionary would hear a groaning sound coming from under a fresh mound of earth. Digging, he would discover an ill Ayore—buried alive. The Ayores believed that for a sick person to die above ground would bring evil on the other members of the tribe and everlasting torment to the person afflicted. Newborn twins, too, were buried alive: the Ayores considered their birth a bad omen, a punishment. To keep twins alive would be to invite terrible consequences from the dark spirit world, and the power of this belief was enormous.

The solution came about in a strange way. The Lord sent a missionary family with twin boys to work among the Ayores. Now the

Indians saw with their own eyes that not having buried their twins alive had not harmed the missionaries. The missionaries were thus able to convince them that burying alive was a meaningless practice. This group of Ayores abandoned it.

The Ayores live in many scattered clans that roam the semidry jungle in southeastern Bolivia—the best estimates place their number at about six thousand. Year by year, one group after the other has been reached. Today hundreds of once-nomadic Ayores are learning farming, reading and writing, house building, medicine and sanitation, and, of course, Christianity; and a few have become church leaders and are even beginning to teach others of their tribe in turn. It is not uncommon for fifty or more Ayores who have never seen a white man to turn up suddenly one day, anxious to learn.

On several occasions, such a group may possibly have come intending to attack the missionaries, too—the Ayores are fiercely warlike—but a combination of prayer and common sense has generally enabled the missionaries to solve this problem.

In one instance, when I was staying in a missionary camp among the Ayores, I heard a commotion a few houses below. Rushing down to learn what it was all about, I saw a number of Ayores, with red and black war paint on their faces, jabbing their spears in the air and grunting angrily as they prepared for battle. When I asked the chief what was going on, he told me a national had killed a tribesman the day before, and they were whipping up the frenzy to go out and attack. "Tomorrow we are going to kill Bolivians," he said. Then he added, "We are fed up with civilization. We may kill you missionaries, too." We missionaries got together hurriedly. This crisis was not something new to us; nevertheless, it was serious. There was no time to do anything but pray, which we did. The Lord answered our prayers: no killing took place.

From my visit, I can realize those five martyrs have not died in vain. Their experience and their inspiration have led to eventual success through the dedication of scores of men and women. And the Ayores are far from being the only example of eventual success.

Let me cite one more tribe: the Pacaas Novos, who live not far from Guajara Mirim. Not long after our work with the Nhambiguaras was halted, Joe Moreno, Tom's father, led a party to try to contact them. (Joe had been with the five missionaries before they were killed by the Ayores. He had escaped death himself only because he was away buying supplies at the time.) The party found a trail of the Pacaas Novos Indians at a riverbank, and paddled across to lay out some gifts. They were greeted by a barrage of arrows and narrowly escaped with their lives by diving into the water.

Three years passed before Joe and his fellow missionaries, after unremitting effort, were at last able to make a friendly contact. From that time on, their progress was rapid. The missionaries established a permanent base deep in Pacaas Novos territory and began the long process of learning the language, then teaching the Indians rudiments of the Gospel. That was almost seven years ago. Today, there are believers among the Indians. Some, like the Ayores, have become missionaries themselves. Over the years the cause has suffered many casualties—missionaries who have had to retire from the battle because of physical or spiritual reverses. But here, as elsewhere, others have come to take the places of the fallen and the reinforcements have outnumbered the losses.

I have seen something else happening among the Pacaas Novos which typifies the pattern of our successes: every group reached tells us of many more tribes whose existence we had not even suspected. A few conversions after years of trying mean much to us; but each beachhead brings news of countless challenges still ahead.

Somewhere I have read that there are an estimated two thousand tribes in the world yet to be reached. From what I have seen for myself in Latin America, this surely is a conservative figure. Flying over the vast green jungles of Bolivia or Brazil has fired my imagination time and again. We are continually spotting new villages, or seeing smoke rising from jungle camps in regions where the existence of wild tribes is unsuspected. Rubber workers, as they penetrate hitherto unexplored areas, bring us reports of new tribes of stone-age men. They come on naked savages as they round a bend in the river; or they see mounds of Brazil nut shells, indications that Indians passed that way. On every hand is evidence of tribes of whom nothing is yet known, not even what to call them.

It is widely assumed that the only frontiers left to our generation are the arctic regions and outer space. True, the areas marked on the map as "unexplored" have greatly shrunk. But this is only because men have flown over them and marked their confines from the air. How many thousands of square miles of jungle remain to be explored in Bolivia alone and how many thousands of square miles more in Brazil, which is eight times as large, to say nothing of the other countries of South and Central America! These jungles contain hundreds of *known* unreached tribes; how many unknown?

The dedicated effort of many missionaries will be required in the years ahead. In unison we cry out for more to come, to be challenged for this work. How often have I pleaded by letter and from behind the pulpit to heed the command, "Go ye into all the world and preach the Gospel to every creature" (Mark 16:15)!

My desire in writing this book has been to portray not only the missionary's struggles, his heartbreaks, emotions, and hopes, but also the strength of his convictions, which lead him to press on, faithful to his promise to God, even unto death.

Once this is understood, it is my hope that people everywhere will become one at heart with the missionary in the job of evangelizing the world.

"Rejoice with them that do rejoice, and weep with them that weep. Be of the same mind one toward another." (Rom. 12:15, 16)

Acknowledgments

Writing this book has been a long and difficult undertaking, with many stops and starts over a period of ten years. I wish to express my appreciation to those who have helped me along the thorny road from the first rough notes in my journal to publication. Especially do I want to thank my friends and fellow workers who gave me the encouragement to go on when I had put it aside, and those in the publishing world who did so much to help me bring my manuscript into final form: Eleanor Jordan of Harper & Row, Edward R. Sammis, consulting editor, and William Carter, editorial assistant.

B. E. P.

Format by Mort Perry
Set in Linotype Times Roman
Composed, Printed and Bound by The Haddon Craftsmen, Inc.
HARPER & ROW, PUBLISHERS, INCORPORATED

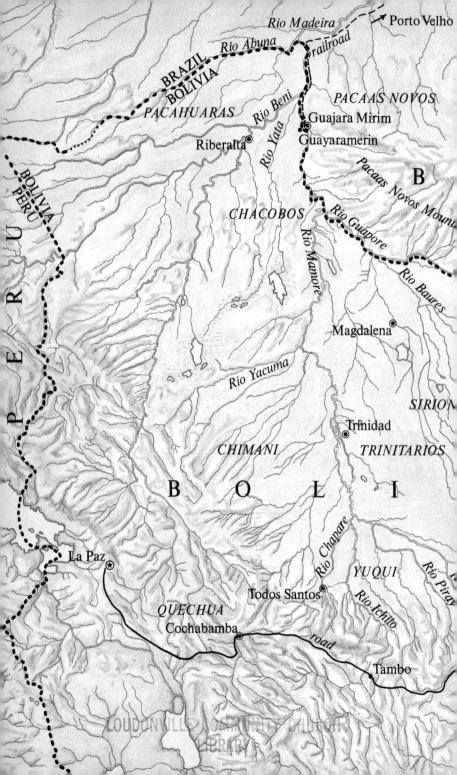